MYSTIC BUTTERFLY

A GUIDE TO YOUR TRUE SELF

JANA PRACKOVA

All rights reserved. No part of this publication may be reproduced, stored in a retrieval system or transmitted, in any form or by any means without the prior permission of the author, nor be otherwise circulated in any form of binding or cover other than that in which it is published and without a similar condition being imposed on the purchaser.

Copyright © 2019 Jana Prackova

First Edition- 2019

ISBN Paperback: 978-1-9993347-0-3
ISBN Ebook: 978-1-9993347-1-0
ISBN Hardback: 978-1-9993347-2-7

Mystic Butterfly® is a registered trademark of Jana Prackova

www.mysticbutterfly.co.uk

Editors:
Alice Cuninghame
Ellie Stevenson

Cover Illustration: Mgr. Maria Lezova

Cover Design: JD Smith Design

Interior Illustrations: Mgr. Maria Lezova

Interior Design: JD Smith Design

Disclaimer

This book is designed to provide information and inspiration to the reader. It is sold with the understanding that within this book, the author and the publisher are not engaged in providing specific legal, medical or other professional services. If such services are required, the reader is advised to contact an appropriate competent professional.

Every effort has been made to ensure that this book is as complete and as accurate as possible. However, the book contains only information available to the author up to the date of first publication. Therefore, the text should be used as a general guide only and not as the ultimate source of information on the subjects covered.

The purpose of *Mystic Butterfly* is to inspire and inform. The author and publisher shall have neither liability nor responsibility to any person or entity with respect to any loss or damage caused, directly or indirectly, by the information contained in this book.

CONTENTS

Introduction	1
Chapter One: Shadow On My Soul	5
Chapter Two: The World Of Sleepers	17
Chapter Three: You Are A Beautiful Mystery	31
Chapter Four: Your Soul And You	41
Chapter Five: The Mysterious World	65
Chapter Six: Cosmic Wonder	83
Chapter Seven: Nature Is My Temple	97
Chapter Eight: And The Darkness Shall Fade Away	111
Chapter Nine: Cosmic Oneness	125
Chapter Ten: Enchanted Wanderland	141
Acknowledgements	153
Recommended Reading	157
About The Author	159

'I would like to dedicate this book to my mum, my dad and my sister. I love you all more than words can ever say'

'The most beautiful experience we can have is the mysterious. It is the fundamental emotion that stands at the cradle of true art and true science.'

Albert Einstein

INTRODUCTION

This is an adventure story. The main character is you, and the adventure is your life. You were born with limitless potential for experience. Since the second you were born, things have happened to, and around you. You've been asked to make choices, take risks or stay safe, do things differently or follow the crowd, work or play. Every choice you make leads to an experience, and every experience becomes another chapter in your adventure story. And your story, just like every story, is unique.

Sometimes, you've found writing your story easy. Your choices are exciting and enticing, you're always learning and trying new things. You relish challenge and change. Sometimes, writing your story is more difficult. You feel tired and lost. Unsure which way to turn, you allow your fear to take over. You try to avoid writing the next chapter. You want to stop, go home and forget about everything. You've had enough of experiences and you've had enough of the story.

Closing the door may allow you to slow the story down, but it will continue to be written. The pen is always in your hand, whether or not you want it to be there. You will have to keep writing the story, and you will write better if you write from a place of understanding.

In this book, you'll gain the understanding you need, to have a life that is meaningful and important. I can't tell you why you're alive, but I can show you how to find and use the tools you need to connect with yourself and the universe. Choose to use these tools, and you'll find that writing your story becomes something you do naturally, easily and with pleasure.

The secrets of fulfilment

All of us want lives that are happy and fulfilled, but achieving these things can seem very difficult. Have you ever wondered what makes some people seem so naturally fulfilled, in a
way that others struggle to be? There's a secret to achieving fulfilment: it comes when you learn to communicate with your soul.

In this book, you'll learn how to communicate with, and look after your soul, your spiritual side. You'll see how you can make your journey through life happy and fulfilling, enabling you to reach a new level of consciousness.

Throughout this book, I'll introduce you to practical tools that you can use to open up possibilities for yourself. These tools will allow you to delve into your soul and communicate with it. You'll learn how to use your intuition as a sixth sense, listening to, understanding and acting on the messages it gives you. You will learn how to meditate, enjoying stillness and the benefits it can bring with just a few minutes a day. As you progress with the reading of this book, you'll discover some magical and mystical secrets of this world. Learning about them will bring many benefits into your life. You may also get answers to some questions you've been curious about, but seem just too uncanny to ask.

By the end of this book, you'll see how to change your perspective on life, and open yourself up to a new adventure that is full of opportunities. By learning to use your thoughts and emotions to create better experiences, you'll be able to take better care of yourself and attract better things.

I will help you learn about the mysteries of the universe, which govern all of us. Understanding these mysteries will allow you to better understand yourself and your experiences. You'll begin to heal yourself, moving on from past wrongs and gaining the future you're meant for.

You have the power to shift your perception, heal yourself, and to inspire those around you and in the wider world, just by being yourself. Your life has a purpose. Let's find it…

CHAPTER ONE

SHADOW ON MY SOUL

On 9th December 2006, I was on a flight to Milan, on which I was working as cabin crew. The flight itself was ordinary, and I had time to relax and chat with a colleague. As we talked, something suddenly changed. The change was subtle at first, a feeling floating into my reality. But before I could think, I felt as if I'd been hit hard in my solar plexus. I became weak, shaky and unable to stand. It felt like all my energy had been sucked out. I wanted to escape, but as I was on a plane, I had nowhere to go. Even if there had been somewhere to go, I didn't have the energy to move.

My colleague was still talking, but I wasn't part of that conversation anymore. I was only an observer of what was going on around me, perceiving it with a foggy sensation on my mind. I felt as if I was watching a dream. That dream quickly became an anxious nightmare, and I became more and more fearful. Through the confusion, I tried to understand why I felt as I did, but I couldn't find an explanation. I struggled through the rest of the flight as best I could.

Once we had landed, I left the aircraft still feeling very weak, and gave myself the time I needed to think about what had happened. I wondered if I'd just been a little tired and stressed. I thought that perhaps I'd had my first panic attack. At that point I all wanted was to sleep, wake feeling refreshed, and forget about the whole thing.

Forgetting wasn't an option. The 'panic attack' on the plane was the start of a long period of unease and discomfort that lasted over four years. That attack on the plane was the first signal I had from my soul that something in my life needed to change. I had a painful and difficult road ahead of me, but I understood for the first time that I needed to explore myself, my reasons for being and the purpose of my life's journey.

A process of change is not always full of light and hope. Every day became challenging. Every day was filled with fear, anxiety and worry. I was constantly questioning where and how I could survive this storm. I was young, in my early twenties, and watching my friends filling their lives with parties and holidays. I couldn't join them. Every morning, I asked myself the question 'how will I get through today?' These were dark days, lived in a shadow that had cast itself on my soul.

It began in childhood

As a child, I had a rich inner life and a vivid imagination. I was artistic and creative, spending my time writing music, stories and poetry. I would often spend many hours composing at the piano. And even from a very

CHAPTER ONE

SHADOW ON MY SOUL

On 9th December 2006, I was on a flight to Milan, on which I was working as cabin crew. The flight itself was ordinary, and I had time to relax and chat with a colleague. As we talked, something suddenly changed. The change was subtle at first, a feeling floating into my reality. But before I could think, I felt as if I'd been hit hard in my solar plexus. I became weak, shaky and unable to stand. It felt like all my energy had been sucked out. I wanted to escape, but as I was on a plane, I had nowhere to go. Even if there had been somewhere to go, I didn't have the energy to move.

My colleague was still talking, but I wasn't part of that conversation anymore. I was only an observer of what was going on around me, perceiving it with a foggy sensation on my mind. I felt as if I was watching a dream. That dream quickly became an anxious nightmare, and I became more and more fearful. Through the confusion, I tried to understand why I felt as I did, but I couldn't find an explanation. I struggled through the rest of the flight as best I could.

Once we had landed, I left the aircraft still feeling very weak, and gave myself the time I needed to think about what had happened. I wondered if I'd just been a little tired and stressed. I thought that perhaps I'd had my first panic attack. At that point I all wanted was to sleep, wake feeling refreshed, and forget about the whole thing.

Forgetting wasn't an option. The 'panic attack' on the plane was the start of a long period of unease and discomfort that lasted over four years. That attack on the plane was the first signal I had from my soul that something in my life needed to change. I had a painful and difficult road ahead of me, but I understood for the first time that I needed to explore myself, my reasons for being and the purpose of my life's journey.

A process of change is not always full of light and hope. Every day became challenging. Every day was filled with fear, anxiety and worry. I was constantly questioning where and how I could survive this storm. I was young, in my early twenties, and watching my friends filling their lives with parties and holidays. I couldn't join them. Every morning, I asked myself the question 'how will I get through today?' These were dark days, lived in a shadow that had cast itself on my soul.

It began in childhood

As a child, I had a rich inner life and a vivid imagination. I was artistic and creative, spending my time writing music, stories and poetry. I would often spend many hours composing at the piano. And even from a very early age, I had a vision that I would one day share my work with the world, sparking passion and conversation.

While I haven't become the famous composer and a singer I once dreamed of being, I have continued to be creative and imaginative. This has shaped my world. Like many creative children, I was introverted, and kept most of my thoughts and feelings to myself. I spent a lot of my time thinking and analysing, and was seen by adults as being old for my years. Partly because I didn't have many friends, I looked inward, to the point of exhaustion. I was strongly affected by criticism, and turned this inward too. Even today, the exact words of the adults in my childhood life, my teachers and parents, echo in my subconscious.

While I was able to understand and appreciate that I was a quiet and creative little soul, I didn't understand the strength of my own intuition, the whispering internal voice that gives us warning messages and signals about things that are yet to happen. I could hear this voice often as a child, and at first, it scared me. I would have a clear understanding that something was about to happen just before it did. As I got used to it, I grew to accept it. Now I understand that this voice is the link between my conscious mind and my soul. I also know that everyone has this voice, but some people have not yet learned to hear it or they simply dismiss it.

As a child, I spoke to my parents about this voice, my intuition. I wasn't to worry about it. I was just experiencing some coincidences, they said. They couldn't have done anything else, as they understood the world only from their own level of perception, which was different to mine. But this disconnection between my own view of the world and everyone else I mentioned it to, meant that I labelled myself as the 'weird kid'.

My intuition led me to the realisation that there must be something higher in the world than that which we can see. While some people believe that it's obvious that when we die, it will be the end of our existence, it was equally obvious to me that this couldn't be the case. It was a concept I couldn't accept, because my daily lived experience told me otherwise. The intuition I had, that guided and protected me every day, was ever-present, and seemed to me to be a clear sign that something existed beyond my immediate physical reality. I would experience constant synchronicities between things that my intuition told me, and things that happened to me, and around me. Where does intuition come from? I wasn't sure exactly, but I knew that it meant that there must be life beyond my physical limits. In my darker moments, I wanted to reject this belief, and become more 'normal'. After a while, I learned to live with my difference, and to keep quiet about it.

As I grew older, I became influenced more and more by my five senses and the physical world. It was, I believed, time to escape my inner world, and experience 'real life' as others did. Other people seemed to move so easily through the world, happy in the immediate present, untroubled by thoughts of what might lie beyond it. I wanted to live easily as they did, and I began to ignore the intuitive inner voice that I used to hear so clearly. I doubted it, and nearly shut it down completely. I stopped believing that there was anything beyond the physical, and set out to live as a normal adult, in the real life that others seemed to prize so highly.

Real life was not as easy to navigate as I had assumed it would be. By trying to join the crowd, I started feeling uneasy and unbalanced. I had learned the rules, but living by them was difficult, even painful. I spent a lot of time trying to please others, hoping that by doing so, they would like and accept me. It was a disappointing and tiring process, as I worked hard to be accepted by people whose truth didn't resonate with my own. I felt lost, and for a long time, I didn't understand why. Then, I boarded that flight to Milan. By the end of that flight, something had changed. I didn't yet know what, but I did understand that I couldn't continue as I had been. It was time to address my fears and search for the way home.

The explosive force of what happened on that flight blew all my blocked emotions out of my core, and up to my consciousness. All the fear, resentment and denial that I'd been living with for years was suddenly, and sharply, present. From my introverted childhood and my teenage attempts to prove I was 'good enough', to my young adult desire to be accepted: they were all there, asking to be dealt with. It was time to understand and make peace with myself. Then, I would be able to start living authentically.

As I set to the task I couldn't ignore, some ugly truths reared their heads. I realised that I'd been living an unhealthy lifestyle, with bad choices that were putting stress on my body and, in turn, blocking my soul's voice. I'd been constantly worrying about others' opinions, criticising myself and making myself fragile.

I'd been expending much of my time and energy on over-analysis and negative thoughts. I'd never made the time to tell myself, as the most important person in my own life, that I loved myself. Though I was having these realisations, my energy was so sapped that I struggled to see a way through. I felt I would need a miracle.

I found that I was often led to thoughts of my childhood and of unanswered questions that had been in my subconscious for all those years. At first, I didn't understand why my childhood experiences were so important, but slowly, I began to see that my childhood self had been my *true* self. By ignoring and stamping down that self, I'd become detached from my soul.

I began to think about the strong intuitive knowings and premonitions I'd had as a child. In remembering them, I remembered who I really was. I understood why I'd spent years feeling lifeless and numb, my physical self wasn't enough. I needed to be more connected to my soul. Without it, I wasn't whole. Together, my body and my soul were my being, and one could not function without the other. The numbness I felt had been a clear signal from my soul that it needed to be looked after. I knew I'd ignored that signal for much too long.

The realisation was liberating, allowing me to begin to uncover my hidden truths. The process of doing so would be fraught with pain and anxiety, but I understood that it was a necessary process. I was not a victim. Those days may have been dark, but I would not take back any one of them. Indeed, I am grateful for them, for they helped me to align with my own truth.

A magical shift

The most painful part of this process I've described began to come to an end when I accepted my feelings. I learned to stop fighting myself and simply accept that the way I was feeling was the right way to feel *at that moment in time*. I didn't need to look into the future, or worry about it. If I still felt the same pain the next day, or the next year, it wouldn't matter. I could accept that the difficult feelings I was having were part of *me*. As they were part of me, I needed to co-operate with them, not fight them. If I fought, I'd be fighting a part of myself. I was scared, I was anxious, I was struggling to sleep. But as I began the process of acceptance, these things started to change. Moments of happiness broke through the worry and fear. Moments became hours, and hours became days. I remember so clearly the day, when I could say: 'today was a great day!' After daily struggle and anxiety, I finally felt I could see my path in front of me, clearer and clearer each day. I had a journey to take and the journey started making more sense.

Like any good traveller, I set about preparing for my journey. At first it wasn't easy, but as I continued, the journey started making more sense. The teachers I needed crossed my path, the books I needed to read came to me, those who would have held me back were led away from me. At times, this was a difficult process. Not all the people who I loved and respected were willing to share my journey with me. Some thought I was mad, some thought I was strange. Others were simply scared of the change they could see me going through. Many of them left my life without explanation.

While this was painful, it is understandable. I was changing, and just as they were not the people I thought they were, so I was not the person they thought I was. Our energies no longer matched. They were not ready to walk the same path as I was. I forgave them and moved on. This was best for all of us, as it meant that they were free to choose the path they felt most comfortable with, and I was able to be fully open to meeting new people. Among those people, were some of the world's best spiritual teachers. With their guidance, I felt liberated, and no longer alone.

I was able to focus on what I needed to do: to become spiritually well. I spent time every day in moments of stillness and reconnection with my true self. These moments allowed me to discover my life's purpose. I knew, at last, why I had been set the challenges I'd had to overcome, why I had experienced so many dark years. I understood that I had a responsibility to share what I had learned. My journey had given me an insight and I knew I could help people learn who they really are, just as I had learnt. I also knew that if enough people came to the same realisations that I had, then there would be a seismic shift in our collective consciousness.

When I began to tell people that I felt I had to share my knowledge and use it to create change, I was initially laughed at, albeit kindly. But I've never wavered. I believe strongly that this is what I'm here to do. Later, many became supportive and started believing in me, because by then I'd fully learnt to believe in myself. In the pages that follow, I'll share my knowledge with you, in the hope that you too will be able to connect with and look after your soul, as I have learnt to do with mine.

Perhaps you're here because you've already spent some time searching for a more spiritual path, or a different kind of connection. Or perhaps, you've never thought much about these concepts before, but something has prompted you to come here. You're in the right place. Read on, and you'll begin to relate to the idea of how to uncover your own truth, communicate with your soul and perhaps even discover your unique purpose. Your soul is half of you, it deserves half your attention, half your time. By giving it that attention, you can move away from and heal your past problems and enjoy a future full of self-expression, and free of false agendas.

There is much to tell you still, much more to the brief story that I've just told you about my life. Throughout this book, you'll be able to read parts of it. But most importantly, I want the rest of the book to be about you, not me. My full story is for another book. In the meantime, I've told it in this poem.

The shadow on my soul

Darkness took over my life…
It had been a painful and frustrating ride.
Living with the shadow on my soul,
unaware of what was wrong and how to get out of it at all.

Suffering every single day and night,
waking up, hoping it would have disappeared overnight.
This was far away from the truth,

I had to go through this painful hurt.

My soul disconnected from my living body,
I felt lost, disorientated, exhausted and uncertain whether I'd wake up in the morning.
Life was a challenge every single day, painful to get through,
I had a feeling it was the end in many ways.

Numbed emotions, not feeling at all, when darkness took over my life
I didn't know what to do, where to turn, how to get 'home'.
Turning to an even more darker side, my wounds were bleeding more and more,
unable to stop the darkness from pulling me away from my soul.

Detached and falling into an even darker hole,
I had lost the connection to my mind, body and soul.
I knew that something needed to change,
I had to find some rescue, liberation and survive this burden in some way.

Not being able to recognise any kind of light,
was keeping me stuck to looking behind.
But one day I realised, acceptance meant letting go,
'If I have to feel like this for the rest of my life, so be it… and I'll go with the flow!'

A sense of liberation lightly touched my body and soul,
and although the wounds were still bleeding,
I felt so much heaviness leaving me and my soul.

This time, it wasn't me who was falling into a darker hole,
but it was the darkness, leaving me, and life gave me another chance to grow.

Grow as a human, a soul and a teacher, to teach and share the light,
my wounds were still bleeding, but life began unfolding in magical ways and was much more bright.
I am so grateful for tasting the darkness for more than a while,
it led me home and made me realise my true purpose and what this life is about.

CHAPTER TWO

THE WORLD OF SLEEPERS

You may have grown up believing that you need to rely on others such as your parents and teachers for knowledge. As an adult, these might become your colleagues, partner, friends, media or the internet. It's certainly true that all of them can offer you valuable insight and learning. But the learning that they can offer you is secondary to the most vital, essential knowledge that you need to live your life authentically. You, and only you, hold the key to the knowledge of your own existence.

Everything in your life that is connected to your presence on this planet, is in your hands. Perhaps you have been searching for answers to important questions such as:

- Why am I here?

- What is my purpose?

- Is there something more to life than working and pay bills?

For as long as I can remember, I have searched for answers to these questions. As I child I found it hard to understand why I had to go to school, why I should learn particular subjects, why I must behave in a certain way at certain times. These rules came without explanation, and seemed nonsensical. I spent a lot of time feeling frustrated and confused with the world.

Eventually, I realised I was looking for answers in the wrong place. They lay *within* me, not outside me. Everything I need to know is inside me. Everything you need to know is inside you.

When you understand that the answers to your important questions lie within you, change will happen, and opportunities will open up to you. If you can become still and listen, you will hear your soul speak. It will give you the answers you seek.

For me, and I hope for you, this realisation has been an awakening, a sunrise after a long, dark night. Colours are brighter, the world is warmer. Existence gains meaning, because the world is no longer in control of you. You create your own reality. In the pages of this chapter, you'll delve into the beliefs that you hold in your subconscious and begin to question them. Some of these beliefs may be serving you well, others may not. You'll learn how to dissolve those that don't contribute to your existence, and build new beliefs and most importantly *'knowings'* in their place that will help you build a more meaningful life. I'll share with you some powerful but simple tools that will allow you to identify and work with your true, powerful self.

Beliefs vs. Truths

For centuries, we humans have adopted the belief that everything worth having is complicated and difficult. Everything good is hard to achieve. This ties into another belief: that we must present ourselves in a certain way in order to be accepted, and to achieve the things we want. These beliefs are ingrained from an early age, and because they are so normal, so common, few of us stop to question them.

We believe many things that other people have told us about ourselves, simply because we have heard the same things many times. After a while these things became part of us. But just because you've been told something many times, doesn't mean it's true.

There is a natural tendency among many people to complicate and over-analyse. It's very easy to worry about things we shouldn't, but doing this simply makes our lives harder, not easier. Most of us, if asked, would say that we want to have an easy, uncomplicated life. Our actions often say otherwise. Our beliefs about ourselves and the world mean that we make sure our lives are difficult and complicated, even though we don't mean them to be. In the school playground, a six-year-old boy says to a six-year-old girl 'you are ugly!' He says this because she annoyed him by getting in the way of his game so he lashes out with the first insult that comes to mind. He doesn't mean it, but the damage is done. Another little girl might have thought nothing of the comment, but this particular little girl believes him. She takes his words deeply into her subconscious. Later, in her thirties, she finds herself struggling with romantic relationships. Those words still ring in her ears.

Let's think about that six-year-old boy now. Without realising it, he said something that will affect that little girl for many years. But he too is affected by the things others say to him, and even by the things they don't. He runs off to play with his friends, and he notices that they're all wearing new, shiny, fashionable shoes. His are old, worn and cheap. Nothing is said to him about his shoes, but he knows they aren't as good as the others. He knows that the shoes are just one more sign amongst many, that his poor family can't compete with other boys' families. He feels he'll never be as good as them. When his friends go to university at 18, he doesn't even apply, even though he has the grades. He doesn't believe he's good enough to have the success that they'll soon come to take for granted.

These beliefs are very powerful, because we've learned them from the most influential people in our lives, our parents and teachers, and public figures via the media. These beliefs have been passed to us down the generations, and we in turn pass them to our own children, and they become part of our culture.

Our culturally ingrained beliefs tell us what we should be, what is right, what is wrong and how we should behave. Many of us accept these cultural beliefs so strongly that they become second nature, and we don't see them as beliefs, but as common sense. We don't see that these ideas come from outside us, not from within, because the lines between the two are so blurred. We're no longer able to identify what is true, and what isn't.

Our cultural, societal beliefs rarely tell us that we should be ourselves. We are bad at teaching our children self-acceptance, and very good at teaching them to fit in. I believe otherwise. It is okay to be yourself. It is okay to express yourself as you are, not as others want you to be. You're the only one of you, there will never be another.

Many people find it difficult to accept themselves as magnificent, wonderful and beautiful. But I accept both myself and you as such. In the pages that follow, I'll continue to remind you of this. You are more than good enough, just as you are.

Perhaps you're now thinking 'I'm not'. Perhaps, now, you want to stop reading this book, because you believe you're not able to be good enough. But remember this, we're all learning and we're all changing. Most of us have done things we regret, and regrets can't always be changed. Don't try to erase your past, instead, work to accept it and to forgive yourself. We're not the same people we were a year ago. We're not the same people we were a month ago, a day ago, even an hour ago. We're constantly changing and growing. Heal your past wounds by making active choices about your future. In the next chapter, you'll learn a powerful technique that will allow you to release yourself from pain and guilt, if you're willing to put in some effort.

We're all doing the best we can with the knowledge and understanding we have, so be gentle with yourself. Strive not for self-punishment, but for greater knowledge and deeper understanding.

JANA PRACKOVA

One of my first false beliefs

I have a clear memory of being in third grade back in Slovakia, and being told by a teacher that I didn't have a mathematical mind. Because the person telling me this was a teacher, someone to be trusted and respected, I didn't question this. It became a fact that I accepted, absolutely. This meant that maths classes became not just difficult, but frightening. So strong was my belief that I had regular nightmares the night before a class, and would go to the class feeling shaky, sweaty and out of control. I can remember a classmate asking me 'how can you live like this? You're worried all the time. It's just school…'

I was shocked that she had noticed, but to me, it wasn't 'just school'. That teacher's comment, which probably meant very little to them, left me less trusting of myself.

As I grew older, other people told me that I couldn't achieve the things I wanted to. The passion for music that I had as a child wasn't enough, I was told, to allow me to develop a musical career. I wasn't good enough. I went to college instead. The subjects at that particular college also included accounting and economics. These weren't subjects that the young, creative, imaginative me was naturally drawn to. They didn't excite me, but I didn't think I had any other choice. These were the things I had to do, because I'd been told I couldn't do anything else. At that time, I believed that pursuing my passions was not a choice I could make.

But, even having made what I thought was the

expected choice, I found myself struggling. The words of that teacher still echoed in my mind, and I found dealing with the mathematical subjects very difficult. I spent many hours preparing for classes, but it never seemed like enough. I was imprisoned by those words said all those years earlier. I don't blame the teacher for the label she gave me. She was acting on her own level of understanding. Like all of us, she was limited and constrained by her own experiences and beliefs. The belief she gave to me was part of her, not me.

It's likely that many or even all of us have said things to people that have had a far greater effect on them than we realised or intended. Rather than blame the people who have unwittingly hurt us, let's acknowledge that we can change ourselves and our outlook. We can come together to speak mindfully and with purpose. When our child fails an exam, let's not punish them, but encourage them and work with them to make them feel better and learn to succeed. When our work colleague makes a mistake, let's not admonish them, but guide them. By recognising that success is often achieved not in giant leaps, but by taking two steps forward and one step back, we'll all be happier and better able to fulfill our potential.

Despite the difficulties I had, I graduated successfully. Looking back, I wasn't as bad at dealing with numbers as I'd thought I was. If I had been, I wouldn't have gained my qualifications. Once college was over, I moved on to new things, and forgot about that terror of maths until in my twenties, when I decided to become a pilot.

I knew that becoming a pilot wouldn't be easy, but

I was determined to achieve it. I was excited by the challenge and started the long process of studying and training to get my private pilot's licence. All was going well, it was hard work, but I felt confident. Then, I started learning navigation, a subject that requires lots of calculations and thorough, detailed flight planning. The old fear of numbers came back. How could I, a person without a mathematical mind, become a pilot? I thought I'd have to give up on my dream. *Then*, I thought again. I gave myself time to relax, and think about my belief that I wasn't good at maths. My desire to be a pilot was stronger than my old belief. For the first time, I began to see it as the view of one person, a long time ago, rather than as a statement of fact about my current abilities. I wanted to learn to fly and be good at it. I wasn't prepared to give that up.

I knew I needed to get past my fear of maths and numbers, so I could pass the navigation section of the course and get my private pilot's licence. I realised I needed to make a decision that I *was* capable of dealing with numbers, I could learn navigation and I could fly a plane. I replaced the old belief that I wasn't capable of doing maths with a belief that *I was capable of doing anything I put my mind to*. Every day of my training, I recited this to myself as an affirmation, over and over. Sometimes, I would say it thousands of times. After a while, this new point of view sank in, and I began to love navigation. I still do. It's a fascinating subject, and one of my favourite parts of flying now.

By shifting my perception, I changed my experience, and I achieved a goal that I couldn't have done before that shift. I'd once thought that 'I'm bad at maths' was an absolute truth for me, but it wasn't. By questioning something I thought was truth, I was able to create a new truth, and that new truth allowed me to achieve my dream.

Think about yourself. Do you have any beliefs that you've failed to question before, but could be holding you back? Identify one belief that has prevented you from achieving something in the past, or is preventing you now. Think carefully about it. What evidence do you have for that belief? Why and when did you start believing it?

Many of us hold limiting beliefs because of something someone else has told us. If your evidence is that other people have told you it's true, consider whether you want to live the rest of your life imprisoned by others' opinions. What is it you really want to do and share with the world? Think of something that makes you *really* excited, something you've always dreamed of doing. Maybe you want to be a pianist, playing to happy crowds in a concert hall. Maybe you want to be a teacher, sharing your knowledge every day with the next generation of children. Maybe you want to be a motivational speaker, inspiring tens of thousands of people around the world. Maybe you want to be a nurse, helping heal injuries and making people feel well again. Whatever your passion, remember you can make it happen.

The choice is yours

I've focused on the limiting belief I had that I was bad at maths but, like most people, I had many others. I have worked, and am still working hard to dissolve them. But having dissolved one belief, I've found that dissolving others is much easier. I now understand that working through change is an essential part of life's journey.

The idea of constant change can be a difficult one to process. There is a comfort in lack of change, but by not changing we block ourselves from progress. If you can accept that your life is to be a process of change, then you will be much closer to living an authentic life. We're always able to reverse past wrongs and undo damaging limiting beliefs. If there is something you believe you can't do, make the decision to believe that you can.

Spend some time now asking yourself these questions:

- What do I believe that may not be true and is controlling me?

- What am I unwilling to let go of?

- What belief do I have that is making my life difficult?

- What scares me most?

- What can I do today to begin to let my fears go?

All of us want to live happy, fulfilling lives, but many of us unknowingly prevent ourselves from leading those happy lives. If you're ready to live the life you want to, the time is now. There's no need or reason to wait any longer. Think of yourself as an artist, painting a picture of your life. You can make the picture whatever you choose, as colourful and vibrant as you want it to be.

Exercise:

Get a paper and pen. Write down all the beliefs you have that you're ready to let go of.

Write down all the things that come to your mind that bother you, and that your life would be easier without.

This exercise will allow you to be honest with yourself, moving beliefs from your head onto the page. Once on the page, they'll be less threatening and less haunting. When you acknowledge that something is not right, you'll start feeling relief. Over time, if you work on dissolving your beliefs, you'll feel lighter, and able to breathe more easily. You may sleep better at night, as there are less difficult thoughts to haunt you. This process of recognising and letting go of beliefs is the most important thing you can do for yourself and your future. It's also the most important thing you can do for others, as you will be free to explore your talents and offer them to the world.

Once you have finished writing your list, write down this statement, on the same piece of paper:

I_____(your name) am ready to release those false and limiting beliefs about myself and my life, and let my true self come forward. I deserve to live a happy and fulfilling life and I am ready to be my greatest self from now on, and forever.

Then, sign it and date it.

Take the list with you to somewhere natural that you feel a connection to. Find a nice, healthy tree, one that feels intuitively right for you, and read your list out loud. When you have finished, bury your list in the ground, at least ten centimeters below the surface.

Say, either out loud or silently:

May all my old beliefs fade away and may my true self come forward.

The earth will begin to start dissolving those beliefs. Your list will disappear into the earth. As this happens, trust and know your life will shift and change. As time goes on, remind yourself every day that you are willing and able to let go of your old beliefs and get ready for new adventures.

If it's difficult for you (as it is for many of us who live in cities and have busy lives) to get out into the natural world, try this alternative. But do it carefully! Take your list, stand above your kitchen sink. Make sure there is nothing flammable nearby, and that your taps work. Set light to your list and burn it, making sure to extinguish it quickly. Flush the ashes away with water. Trust and know that the element of fire has started the process of dissolving your old, limiting beliefs.

A thought to keep

False beliefs and labels cause us to live in fear and worry, depression and scarcity. By letting go of them, we allow ourselves a joyful existence.

CHAPTER THREE

YOU ARE A BEAUTIFUL MYSTERY

Many people believe that we are all solely, or at least mainly, physical beings. We work, we earn, we strive for success. That success is measured in qualifications, houses and possessions, and we work hard for these things. We want to create a comfortable world for ourselves and our children. We do all of this because we want to feel happy and fulfilled, and often, we do feel like that.

But there is often a price to be paid for our achievements. Working hard, striving to pay a mortgage and increase our wealth means considerable sacrifice. We're often unable to spend the time we would like to spend with our loved ones, and lack the freedom we need to spend on ourselves and our passions. Many of us are left, after a stressful day at work and a long commute, thinking 'is this all there is?'

There *is* more in life to enjoy and explore. All of us are able to open ourselves to an adventure. Inside you lies your own mystery. Can you sense it? Perhaps you already feel that there is something more around you and within you than your physical being. Perhaps you don't feel it yet, but in this chapter, you'll learn how to, by communicating with your inner self.

Most of our communication is with the world outside of ourselves or perhaps in our minds. The true inward communication is often difficult, and doesn't come naturally. Once you master the art of inner communication, you'll be able to experience your whole self, and lead a more meaningful and colourful life. In the previous chapter, we talked about how false, limiting beliefs can hold you back from achieving the things you want. In this chapter, you'll learn more about how to release yourself from your past, look forward rather than behind, and build a happy future that feeds not only your five senses, but your need for inner peace.

This is an exciting path to take. If you're new to this kind of conversation, take a deep breath. Walk through the pages that follow with an open mind and heart. If you've already begun your spiritual journey, you'll sharpen your connection to your inner self. You'll be amazed at what you learn.

Your highest identity

Take a look in the mirror. You'll see your physical being, and that is part of you. But which part is observing what you see in the mirror? That is your soul. Together, they are united as one whole, to form everything you are. Your soul and your body co-operate with each other, working together to create beautiful things. In so doing, you also create a beautiful space for other souls entering this dimension in the future, preparing the ground for them to fulfill their dreams and their purpose.

I believe that we are infinite universal beings currently expressing ourselves us humans. Our souls inhabit our human bodies in order to have an experience that we can learn from and evolve from. In our bodies our souls can experience touch, taste, smell, hearing and sight. We are here to learn as much as we can about this reality, and in doing so we prepare the ground for other souls to come and fulfill *their* plans.

If you're able to learn, as I will teach you, how to live an authentic life, you'll benefit others as well as yourself. When you live an authentic life, you live your own truth to its fullest. Your own truth is yours to define. For me, it's that I don't need to pretend to be someone else in order to be accepted. I can be myself, confidently and completely. I can say things that resonate with me, without worrying about whether they are the things others want to hear. It means loving myself fully and sharing my truth with the world. It is the most liberating experience anyone can have.

Most of us have not had the meaning of our souls explained to us. We don't discuss this in school, or talk about it with work colleagues. Only when we hit a crisis do we begin to ask questions. When we feel lost and lonely, we look for answers. When we fail to find answers in the physical world, we turn to the spiritual, feeling that we have nothing to lose by doing so.

We look at ourselves as inhabitants of the earth, as individual humans and as part of humanity. All those things are true, but they are not all there is. Our souls are just as important. Without our souls, our physical beings would not exist. The two halves are co-dependent, and by connecting better with our soul, we can even improve our physical health. I believe that when our soul is well, we also feel physically well. Our souls play a huge role in our physical bodies. They try to communicate with us and encourage us, even when we don't want to listen. When waiting for the results of a medical test, we often fear the worst, even when our inner wisdom may be whispering, 'don't worry, nothing is wrong, be calm'. In this way, we waste our precious energy and valuable time. If we can learn to hear that voice and co-operate with it, we can save our energy and use it for something positive and meaningful.

All of us, even if we're not aware of it, have made some connection between our physical bodies and our souls. But for many of us the connection is very weak, so weak that we quickly dismiss it. Learn to make and feel that connection, allow your body and soul to communicate better, and you'll experience huge change. Your own consciousness will shift, and so will our collective consciousness. There are many ways in which you might feel the effects.

You're likely to start seeing obstacles as opportunities. You'll see that worry is futile, and become able to set it aside. You'll become aware that your reality is created by your thoughts and emotions and you'll take steps to change them. Learning about your true identity, *being partly human, partly soul* will bring some wonderful benefits into your life. It will make this journey for you so much more interesting and very exciting.

Shifts in consciousness begin with small changes. You can start today. Become mindful of your thoughts, actions and interactions. Think about where you direct your energy, and work to set an example to others. By being the best version of yourself you can be, you can create an amazing shift in your consciousness.

Intuitive messages and feelings

In my understanding, intuition is the link between our soul and our physical being. Often, we choose to ignore the things it tells us, explaining them away as coincidental, rather than meaningful. We have a premonition that something important is about to happen, and we pass it off as random chance. As a child, I often knew what someone was going to say before they said it, or would think of something and it would appear shortly after. One day, I was on the school bus and an image flashed into my mind. I saw the local shop repainted from its usual white to red, white and blue overnight. The bus swung around the corner and stopped opposite the shop, which was painted exactly as I had visualised it. I felt scared because I didn't understand how I could've known this. I told friends, and they dismissed it as coincidence. I learned to stay quiet and ignore my 'weirdness'. Now, I understand that I was using my intuition, a powerful gift from my soul that is to be treasured, not pushed away.

The spiritual world is often unknown and unexplainable. We can't always experience it through our five senses because it vibrates on a different frequency to our own. But by working to raise our vibration, we can begin to experience the spiritual world in some form. It's constantly giving us signs and warnings. It's able to give us the answers to our most important questions, if only we're able and willing to listen.

When you learn more about your soul and how to communicate with it, you'll see these signs, warnings and answers everywhere. Perhaps you'll see a billboard with words that provide an answer you've been looking for. Maybe you'll see feathers on the ground every day as you walk to work, a sign that the angels are protecting you. You might have a bad feeling about a new colleague, a warning that they're not to be trusted. Or an old friend might let you down, a warning that something has changed in your relationship.

There's a good chance that up to now, you've been able to dismiss the voice of your soul. Most of us do, because we've never been taught what it is. You've been living your life, concentrating on gaining an education and a career, and busy developing your family and social life. All these are important things to do, but they're not *everything*. Are you ready to make a deeper connection with the other side of your being now? Let's do that.

Communicating with your soul

Communicating with your soul may look like a major task. Perhaps you're thinking of Buddhist monks, silent in meditation, and believe you can't do the same. You don't need to. Communicating with your soul does take a certain amount of practice and discipline, but it's easier than you think. In fact, you're already communicating, you may just not be aware of it.

I believe, meditation is one of the easiest ways to begin to acknowledge this connection. Some people think meditation is difficult, or it must follow a particular format. In contrast, meditation can be anything you'd like it to be. It might be sitting in stillness in your favourite chair. It might be walking in the fields, connecting with the natural world. It might be observing the flicker of a candle flame, or the way the clouds float in the sky. Meditation allows you to become fully present in the moment, undistracted by the past and future. It is stillness of the mind, the ability to forget your worries and even the fact that you're meditating. It's a shift out of the fictional scenarios that your mind creates, and into the pure bliss of the present moment. With regular practice, you'll learn to reach deep into yourself. You'll hear your intuition: the voice of your soul. By 'hear', I don't mean a physical hearing, but a knowing. It's something that must be experienced to be understood, because your logical mind will always fail to explain it.

The present moment is a wonderful place to be. The past has gone, and can't be changed. Our approach to it can be changed, but not the events of the past. If we live in the past, we limit our connection to the present. The future is not yet here, and while it's good to plan for and enjoy thinking about the future, over-thinking it can restrict your plans, rather than help you make them.

If you're willing to trust the universe, via your instinct and your intuition, you'll find that it will create the best possible outcomes for your personal and spiritual growth. The possibilities are unlimited, so be open to them. Allow the universe to take care of you and your future. I believe that everything has divine timing and purpose, and life unfolds exactly as it's supposed to. You and your soul are on an adventure, and your soul is tirelessly providing navigation. But your human mind is often louder than your soul's voice, and it tries to control your journey without understanding it. The soul does understand. It knows that there is a time for everything, and that when one thing doesn't work, something else will. It understands that life will unfold as it should, when the time is right.

Let your soul navigate. Be fully in the present, and allow yourself to meditate and communicate with your soul. Meditation is one of the easiest ways to begin communicating with your soul.

A simple meditation for beginners

Find a comfortable place, somewhere you won't be disturbed for at least five minutes. You can even choose to meditate somewhere outdoors, in a natural environment. Sit down, and make sure your feet are planted firmly on the ground. Close your eyes so that you're not distracted by anything outside of yourself.

Take a deep breath through your nose and exhale through your mouth. Breathe very slowly and deeply, with your exhalation longer than your inhalation. Do five rounds of inhalation and exhalation. You should begin to feel more centred, and ready for the next step.

As you take another breath in, imagine you are breathing in a pure white light. This light represents all of the positive energy in the universe. As you breathe out, visualise your fears and worries. Let go of any thoughts that are not serving you well. I call these negative emotions 'clouds of darkness'. Visualise these clouds travelling far away into the distance. They have gone, and will never come back. Repeat this cycle of breathing in and out five times. Then, slowly return your breathing to its normal pace. Keep your eyes closed, and visualise your surroundings. Become aware of where you are and of your body. When you are ready, open your eyes. Take your time to get up and get on with your day.

You've just meditated. How did you find it? Could you make this simple meditation part of your daily routine? If you can, you're on your way to enriching your life. I have found that my daily meditation practice has changed the quality of my life for the better. I've become a much calmer person. I've stopped trying to control outcomes, approaching each situation with an open mind. I've learned to breathe better, pausing several times a day to check that I am breathing slowly and deeply. When I find myself rushing, I know I need to stop and take a deep breath. I'm more energised and creative. I'm happier.

Make a commitment to yourself that you will meditate every day for 10 days (and I would be very surprised if you didn't want to continue after the 10 days are up). When you're ready, add more time to the meditation, and continue to build it as time goes on.

In the chapters to come, I will give you more powerful tools and rituals that you can use for the rest of your life. If you, like most of us, have unhealthy or unproductive habits that you would like to stop, these rituals can become a substitute for those habits. You'll be able to stop reaching for a drink every time you have a bad day, comfort eating when you feel unfulfilled, or going shopping when you feel down. All of us have our own unproductive habits, and all of us can stop them if we choose.

You will also find that your intuition will come to the surface more often, allowing your soul to be that powerful part of your being it truly is. Your wounds will start to heal and your perspective on your life will shift.

CHAPTER FOUR

YOUR SOUL AND YOU

As you've read this book, you've learned to see your soul as part of you. Your body is here, physically anchored in our everyday world. Your soul shares your body's journey for as long as your body is on earth. When your body is gone, your soul will move on with its journey. I see the soul as a Mystic Butterfly: beautiful, inspiring and adventurous. It travels the universe, taking on various forms. At this moment in time, it has chosen to take on a physical life by becoming you.

Your soul needs to be nurtured also, as you nurture your body. Maybe you make an effort to eat well, play sports and take long country walks. All these things are fantastic for your body and mind, but alone, they won't give your soul all the nourishment it needs. Perhaps you also practise yoga, or make a conscious effort to take in the natural world around you when you walk. These things will benefit your soul, but it still needs a little more to be truly healthy and balanced.

How your soul and body connect

You have a body. This is made up of organs, millions of cells, water and many other complex parts. Each part of your body works with the others to make sure everything functions the way it should. Your soul is made up of chakras. These also work together, helping each other and making sure everything functions as it should. I see chakras as the 'organs' of the soul. The chakras are centres through which energy flows. Understanding them is vital to understanding and nourishing the soul. In this chapter, you'll learn some basic information about them, how to strengthen them, and why.

Your chakras and the aura

The word chakra comes from the ancient Indian Sanskrit, and means *spinning wheel of energy*. These vortices of energy interact with your physical, mental, emotional and spiritual body to create harmony. For a healthy soul you need healthy chakras, just as for a healthy body you need healthy organs. One interacts with the other on a deeper level.

The chakras are like rainbow-coloured dots stretched horizontally along the spine (see the picture below). The chakras distribute energy throughout your body. Although they are invisible to most of us, some people can see them. There are people with the ability to perceive the world beyond their five senses, such as healers or shamans. You too can *awaken* this ability, if you're open to it. All of us can sense energy around us and easily pick up on vibes from others. If you can do this, you're able to sense chakras. We're all powerful souls with many fantastic gifts and abilities yet to be discovered. Chakra colours are fluid and changing as your emotions change and they can become muddy and faded. The colours of the chakras indicate your current state (physical, mental, emotional, spiritual).

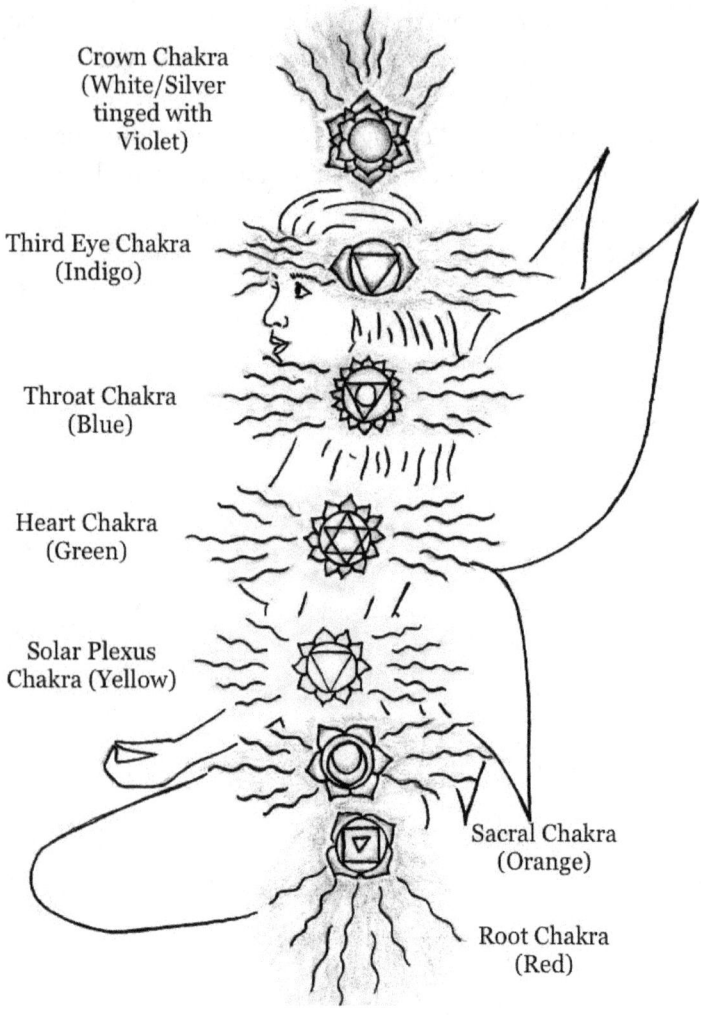

The energy of your chakras extends out of your soul, creating an energy field around you called an aura. The aura is the connection between your soul and your body, between the physical and the ethereal. The aura is not static, but ever-changing, responding to everything we do. It reflects our feelings and our physical and spiritual health.

All living beings have auras. The aura is like a halo, of the kind you've seen on angels or other sacred figures in religious paintings. But unlike the halo, the aura surrounds your entire being. The aura can also be defined as an invisible field of everything which hasn't yet manifested physically. Your entire state is represented by your aura. Your aura has many layers, the most well-known of which are the first seven layers that correspond with each chakra. You can see these in the picture below. If there's an imbalance in a chakra, this is reflected in the aura. When the imbalance reaches the aura layer which corresponds to that particular chakra, it will also be reflected in the physical body. Your aura is connected to your personality, thoughts, and well-being (physical, mental, emotional and spiritual). It changes its colours based on how you feel, or what you're going through in life, but the dominant colour of your aura doesn't change.

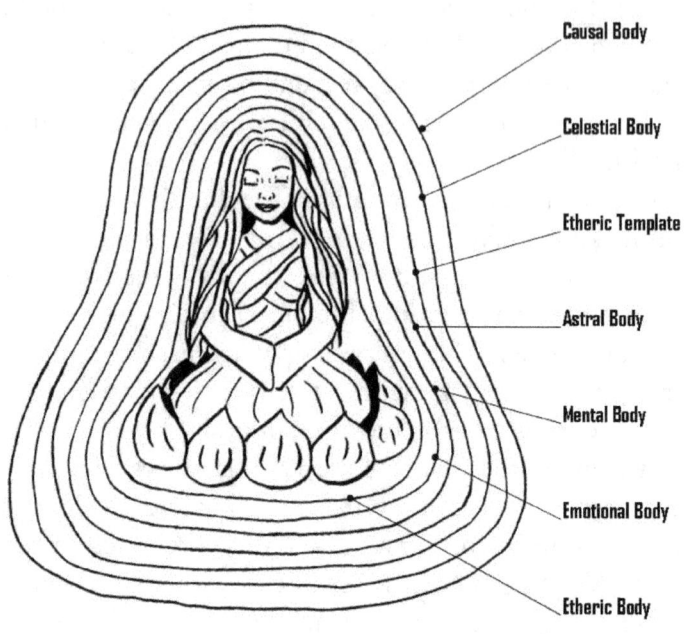

Chakras and auras influence each other, with chakras being internal and auras external. If one of your chakras isn't in harmony, this will be reflected in your aura. Your aura represents what radiates from your chakras.

How I discovered chakras

At the beginning of the book, I told you the story of my flight to Milan, and the violent, invisible punch I felt, that drained my energy and brought me to the realisation that I had to make changes in my life. I felt, physically, the disconnection between my body and my soul. I was lifeless, as if I was functioning on autopilot, unable to influence my own direction.

At the time, I didn't understand what was happening, but I did know that I was missing something. I had no idea what it was, but I knew I needed something else if I was to feel complete. I didn't realise at first, that the feelings I was experiencing were a message from my soul to re-evaluate my life. Now I know that at that time, my soul was struggling to hold me together. It didn't want to let me give up. It knew that if it could find a way to communicate with myself better, I would be able to find a better path for myself.

My soul has become a vital source of guidance and support for me. It encourages me when I feel down and gives me the strength I need to get up in the morning, even when I don't want to. It reminds me why I'm here. Sometimes, I sense that my soul is tired, but even then, it never lets me down. I know that it's my responsibility to look after my soul as best I can, in return for everything it does for me.

After my experience on the plane to Milan, I began my search for fulfilment. While I didn't realise it at first, my soul became my guide on that search, sending me teachers, healers, books and wisdom when I needed them. Eventually, I realised that none of this was coincidence. With the voice of my soul becoming louder and louder, I began to listen.

During this time, I came across the ancient Indian teachings on the chakras. I was instantly fascinated by the idea of these invisible energy centres, and felt compelled to research them. The whole concept felt familiar to me, even though I was reading about it for the first time. It helped me to understand some of the experiences I'd started noticing in my childhood and also my desire to find a connection. I realised that we're much more than we believe. All of us have a huge amount of power, but sadly most people never realise the extent of their power. It's only by understanding and acknowledging our being as a whole that we can do so.

Once I understood this, I could never go back to the way I was before. I could never again ignore my own unlimited power. This was a liberating feeling, but at times it was also confusing. Sometimes, I wasn't sure what path I should follow and I could feel myself becoming distracted. If, on your own journey, you can feel this happening to you, don't give up. Keep reading and keep learning. As you discover how to look after your chakras, you'll discover how to live the fulfilling life that you want.

As a child, I was fully aware how my body responded to my emotions. When I felt lacking in confidence, I experienced discomfort in my stomach. When I felt scared to speak up, I felt tightness in my throat. These days, as I gather knowledge about chakras from my studies, my teachers and my spiritual work with people, I pick on chakra imbalances within myself and others. These are reflected in the behaviour, patterns, physical and emotional issues we experience.

When your soul speaks

I often visit theatres and concert halls and when I do, I notice that people in the audience often spend time clearing their throats, coughing and fidgeting. This is annoying, but I believe I understand why it happens. People who are drawn to these places are often artists and musicians, and they want to express themselves in a musical or creative way. When they visit places like these and are surrounded by what they love, their throat chakra gives them a signal to express themselves too. They start clearing their throat chakras by coughing even without realising what they're doing.

One day, during a performance at the Royal Albert Hall I noticed this throat-clearing and coughing happening. I mentioned my theory to my friend. Being open to this kind of conversation, he agreed, instantly amazed and fascinated by the point I was making.

Our souls constantly give us signals and let us know through our chakras that something is unbalanced and needs to be healed. This is expressed physically in our bodies. When this happens, our initial reaction is often to numb the discomfort using an external solution, such as medication. But our souls want us to go inward and listen to the guidance they're giving us. Our minds, which have been trained and programmed to dismiss our soul's voice, take over and start looking for outside solutions.

After the unpleasant experience I had on the plane to Milan I began to feel a burning sensation in my lower back. I felt it daily for a few years, and it was mostly noticeable when I was deep in fear, or when I felt unsafe or insecure. Now I know my root chakra but also my sacral chakra, were both responding to an imbalance. I was ungrounded and didn't feel safe anywhere. I wasn't expressing myself creatively enough and held lots of emotions inside. I often felt I needed to escape somewhere, but I had nowhere to go.

Once, I had a big panic attack at a restaurant. I was sitting there with a friend, and everything around me seemed to be in a slow motion. I couldn't breathe and my heart was pounding. I felt shaky and I thought that at any minute I'd lose my mind and die. I ran outside, thinking I might be able to breathe better out there, but it didn't help. I managed to get home as quickly as I could, but the unpleasant feelings were still there. They didn't go away until I fell asleep. I had similar anxiety attacks most days, for years. They could happen anywhere: at home, in the park, on a plane or in the cinema. The burning sensation in my lower back made me feel out of control and extremely scared, every time. Later, when I began reading and learning about the chakras, it began to make sense. I discovered how ungrounded I was. As I began my research and eventually started taking classes and courses, everything was clearer. I learnt how important is to communicate with my soul. I realised my soul cannot function without my body, and vice-versa. A misalignment in one influences the other. When I take care of my soul the way I take care of my body and mind, I become balanced and grounded. I feel whole.

Beginning your own research

You too can begin your own research and learn how to communicate with your soul. You don't have to go through what I did to begin the adventure that happens when you get to know yourself on a deeper level. Chose to nourish your being as a whole and this will be reflected on the outside and the inside.

There are many different ways: teachers, healers and ancient texts all talk about the chakra system. Many books and articles have been published on the subject and sometimes give opposing viewpoints. None of them are wrong, because truth is perception. Even what I'm writing about in this book is based on *my* understanding and the intuitive guidance I've gained from my own soul. It's the information I've learnt from my teachers, the books I've read and my own observations while working with people. I ask you to follow *your* intuition (as you're learning to acknowledge it more now) and use whatever feels right for you. If something doesn't feel right, let it go. This is *your* adventure and your own path towards your true self.

The chakras: anatomy of a human soul

Most of the literature you'll read about chakras will teach you that there are seven of them. This is a simplification: there are many more than these seven. But it is the seven primary chakras that are the core of your soul, and it's these you need to understand first.

1. The Root Chakra
2. The Sacral Chakra
3. The Solar Plexus Chakra
4. The Heart Chakra
5. The Throat Chakra
6. The Third Eye Chakra
7. The Crown Chakra

There are three earth chakras, the Root, Sacral, Solar Plexus chakras, that keep us grounded to the earth and able to experience our physical life. There are three spirit or sky chakras, the Throat, Third Eye and Crown chakras, that provide our link to the rest of the universe. The connection point between the earth and the spirit or sky chakras is our Heart chakra. This is the centre of love and kindness. Love is the most powerful force in the universe. When you act from a place of love, you activate a beautiful energy which influences everyone and everything around you. This creates a magical healing that benefits us all.

The seven primary chakras

Below I've summarised each chakra so you have a guide to refer to whenever you need a reminder. Each chakra is represented by a specific colour that follows the colours of the rainbow. These colours are fluid and change as your emotions change, but every chakra has a particular dominant colour.

You'll see that for each chakra I've included an affirmation. This is something that you can repeat to yourself whenever you feel you need to. If you feel that a particular chakra is becoming unbalanced, repeat the affirmation to re-centre and focus.

1) The Root Chakra

Location: the base of the spine

Colour: red

What it does: creates a connection to the physical world. It is the centre of our stability, security and trust

What happens when it's unbalanced? You become fearful, anxious and untrusting

Keywords: 'I am'

Affirmation: I am safe, secure and supported at all times

2) The Sacral Chakra

Location: below the navel

Colour: orange

What it does: encourages creativity, sexuality and sensuality

What happens when it's unbalanced? You lack energy and become de-motivated, sad, and depressed.

Keywords: 'I feel'

Affirmation: I am creative and inspired

3) The Solar Plexus Chakra

Location: between the belly button and the heart

Colour: yellow

What it does: inspires confidence, power, self-development and willpower

What happens when it's unbalanced? You feel stressed and unable to concentrate, as if you have lost your centre

Keywords: 'I do'

Affirmation: I am calm and confident

4) The Heart Chakra

Location: the heart

Colour: *green*

What it does: *inspires love, compassion and empathy*

What happens when it's unbalanced? *You find it hard to trust or forgive and become apathetic and uncommitted*

Keywords: *'I love'*

Affirmation: *I am loving and compassionate*

5) The Throat Chakra

Location: the centre of the throat

Colour: blue

What it does: develops communication and truthful expression

What happens when it's unbalanced? You feel isolated, anxious, nervous and fearful. You're afraid of your own truth

Keywords: 'I speak'

Affirmation: I speak my truth and I express myself fully

6) The Third Eye Chakra

Location: the middle of the forehead, between the eyebrows

Colour: dark blue or indigo.

What it does: develops intuition, awareness and the search for wisdom

What happens when it's unbalanced? You suffer from headaches and nightmares

Keywords: 'I see'

Affirmation: I trust my soul and I listen to my intuition

7) The Crown Chakra

Location: the top of the head

Colour: this chakra is often visualised as violet (I teach to visualise it as white/silver, tinged with violet)

What it does: aids spirituality and a connection to higher consciousness

What happens when it's unbalanced? You become confused and depressed and lack faith in yourself and the world

Keywords: 'I understand'

Affirmation: I am one with all that is and I create my reality

Looking after your chakras

Each of these chakras is important. Each is vital to your well-being. They need you to take the time to nurture and nourish them.

Meditation is vital to keeping chakras healthy, balanced and in harmony. Practise it daily and you will begin to see shifts in the way you experience the world.

Below, you'll find a meditation I use, for myself and with my clients, to balance chakras. The first part of the meditation will take you into a mental space where you feel balanced and connected. The second part of the meditation is designed to work on balance for each chakra individually.

Note: I suggest you read this meditation a few times first, before you put it into practice. You can also access this meditation on my website at www.mysticbutterfly.co.uk/meditation

Your chakra meditation

Make yourself comfortable. Have your back straight, relax your shoulders and arms, letting your hands rest on your lap. Close your eyes to avoid distractions. Very slowly, start taking deep, long breaths. When you breathe in, imagine that you are breathing in a pure, white light. This light represents positive energy. When you exhale, imagine you are breathing out dark clouds. These clouds represent your worries and fears. Repeat this five times, and then return your breath to its natural pace.

Now think about your connection to the earth. Visualise that connection. Roots grow through your feet and keep you grounded. You are supported, safe and secure. A beam of beautiful light shines up from your head, connecting you to the rest of the universe. You are connected to all that there is, from above and below. Appreciate this. Take another long, deep breath to make the connection stronger. Keep breathing. Relax.

Root Chakra

Imagine a beam of vibrant red light at the base of your spine. As you breathe in, this light expands in all directions of time and space and the colour red gets even more vibrant. Breathe out, and visualise any negative feelings you have leaving your body. The earth is absorbing these feelings and turning them into positive energy that cannot cause harm to you or others. Keep on breathing. See the light growing brighter as you become more grounded and supported.

Sacral Chakra

Imagine a beam of orange light coming in from just below your belly button. Breathe in, and feel the light expanding in all directions of time and space and becoming brighter. Breathe out and imagine a waterfall of energy washing away negative feelings and worries. Every time you breathe out, your chakra becomes purer and clearer. Take another deep, long breath and release.

Solar Plexus Chakra

Imagine a beam of yellow light coming from the upper part of your belly. The light expands in all directions of time and space and becomes brighter with each breath. When you breathe out, any energy that no longer serves you is released. Imagine this energy travelling into the far distance, to be dissolved by fire. The fire transforms it into pure, positive energy that can do no harm.

Heart Chakra

Imagine an emerald green beam of light coming from your chest. As you breathe, this light is expanding in all directions of time and space, and any negative feelings that prevent you from loving or being compassionate begin to be dissolved. Feel unconditional love around your being. Keep breathing. Release feelings that you don't want to have anymore. See these feelings being carried far away by the air. They will never return, but will be turned into light.

Throat Chakra

Imagine a beautiful beam of blue light coming from your throat. Imagine it expanding in all directions of time and space, and clearing away anything that stops you from being truthful or expressing yourself honestly. See these restrictions leaving from your throat, turning into positive energy. Now, you are beginning to awaken to your truth and the reason you came here.

Third Eye Chakra

Imagine a beam of indigo light coming from your forehead. This light expands your awareness, reaching all directions of time and space and clearing away anything that stops you from connecting to the spiritual world. Anything that doesn't resonate with your truth is released. Breathe very deeply, and as you breathe out, feel the blocks to truth melt away. Your connection to the spiritual world is expanding.

Crown Chakra

Imagine a beam of white/silver light tinged with violet shining from the top of your head. As you breathe slowly, this light expands in all directions of time and space. When you breathe out, imagine anything that restricts you leaving from the top of your head. As you keep breathing, you feel purer and more balanced. You feel yourself. As you keep breathing, you are supported by cosmic energy which will help you understand your mission on earth.

Keep taking slow and deep breaths. Now, it's time to close your chakras. Close each of them to the size that feels right for you. Visualise this process as flowers closing their petals at night. Starting with the crown chakra at the top of your head, work down to the root chakra, at the base of your spine.

Keep breathing slowly and deeply. Feel your connection with the universe. Your chakras are now more balanced and in harmony. You are grounded and supported. Only love and light radiates from you, surrounding and protecting you.

When you are ready, slowly become aware of your body. Stretch. When you feel comfortable, open your eyes. Take your time getting up and have a glass of water afterwards to purify your body.

Using chakra balancing in your everyday life

You can use this meditation every day, or at least every day that you can. This is a very powerful way of connecting with the spiritual side of your being. The more you practise this meditation, the more you will get to know yourself on a deeper level. Take your time working on each chakra. Take as many deep breaths into the space each chakra is in as you feel you need. Only move to the next chakra when you are ready. You will, slowly but surely, be able to recognise misalignments and unbalanced chakras intuitively. You probably recall from Chapter Three that intuition is the link between your physical self and your soul. It's the powerful knowing, either that something isn't right, or that you feel you can trust. Intuition is the internal voice which gives you the access to the world beyond your five senses, a world you're beginning to discover by reading this book.

Activities you can do to keep your chakras balanced

Beside meditation, there are many activities you can do to balance, strengthen and heal your chakras. You can connect with the natural elements of earth, water, fire and air, of which more in Chapter Seven. You can harmonise your chakras with crystals and healing stones, something I highly recommend you research. Practising yoga or any other physical exercise can strengthen your chakras and create a healthy aura. Some healers recommend wearing clothes in the colour of whichever chakra is unbalanced. Eating healthy, organic fruit and vegetables of the same colour as each chakra can be a good way to contribute to an awakening and healing of your spiritual self.

Below are a few more suggestions for you. Try them out and experiment. See what works for you and what you're intuitively drawn to.

The Root Chakra

To feel grounded and connected to the earth, try gardening, spending time in, and meditating in the natural world, physical exercise, yoga.

The Sacral Chakra

Long baths, swimming, walking by the sea or river, massage, creative work, painting, dancing, yoga.

The Solar Plexus Chakra

Self-development activities that help increase your confidence, reading, being open to the sun's power by getting out more often on a sunny day, lighting candles.

The Heart Chakra

Nature walks, spending time with loved ones, hugging (even hugging yourself), having plants around your home, listening to soothing music, meditation.

The Throat Chakra

Sound healing such as singing, expressing yourself creatively (writing poetry, painting, composing music), having meaningful conversations with friends, keeping a journal of your ideas.

The Third Eye Chakra

Getting out in the evening and gazing at the stars, meditating under the stars, being open to other perspectives on the world.

The Crown Chakra

Focusing on your dreams and visions, meditating.

This chapter has given you an understanding of the anatomy of your soul and how to start looking after it. You are getting to know yourself better, and starting to experience the benefits your being longs for, and deserves. Heathy chakras create a healthy aura, and this will always be reflected in your entire being: physically, mentally, emotionally and spiritually.

In the next chapter I will tell you about the infinite

spiritual guidance which is available to you and ready to assist you at any time. You'll discover that you're not alone and that there is much in your favour in this universe.

CHAPTER FIVE

THE MYSTERIOUS WORLD

All of us are able to access spiritual guidance when we want and need it. Our guides are celestial beings: angels, spirit guides and deceased loved ones. They exist to protect us and help us. This knowledge is liberating and confidence-giving. It means that you know there is always something there for you, drawing your attention to things you need to know, to warnings, messages and signs. Every one of us can see these if we want to, but few of us do. It's easy to label them as coincidences and simply dismiss them. If you're able to understand and respond, you'll be able to live a happier and more fulfilled life. In this chapter, I'll show you how to do it and explain why it's important.

Ever since I discovered I'm not alone in the universe, I've been able to relax into life. I trust that if I ever feel stuck, confused or demotivated, my guides will be there to help. This is liberating. I know that I'm always protected, with signs and synchronicities shown to me to guide me. Many of my old worries and fears have dropped away with the knowledge that I'm not alone.

No one is alone. You are not alone. All of us can be guided by the mysterious world, even those who choose not to believe this is possible. Your spirit guides are with you and ready to help you at any time. To benefit from their guidance, all you need to do is ask for it. Read this chapter and be comforted. Even when the times are hard there is much in your favour.

It's uncanny...

Ever said that? Most of us have. You may not have paid much attention at the time, but think back now. Can you remember a time when something happened that you already knew would happen? Many people become anxious or worried when they think about this. Many others feel uncomfortable with talk of the spirit world, unsettled by it. But don't worry. Keep reading. Any fear you have now is understandable, but be open. Stay with me until you understand more.

I believe that there are many levels of existence. There are other galaxies, other dimensions and parallel worlds. We can't see these with our eyes, but we can feel them. They operate on a different frequency to our world. To be able to experience them or at least feel them, we need to change our frequency so that it matches theirs. You can do this yourself, with a little guidance and practice.

First, simply allow yourself to be aware of these other worlds and the other beings within them. They are there and can help you at any time you need them. Start with awareness, and communication will grow. Remember that we are only looking for communication. The beings you communicate with will not interfere with your free will. They will give you signs, and it's up to you whether you follow or ignore those signs. You will always have free will.

Free will

Everyone has free will. When you came to this planet, you had free will. You still do. You, and only you, decide what you want to do and experience. You make choices for yourself. Choices can lead to mistakes, but despite this, your spirit guides and angels will never interfere with your free will. They want you to have your own experiences, that you create. They want you to learn lessons from your reality, which sometimes means you will have to do things you don't enjoy.

We all do things we don't enjoy sometimes, but this particularly applies to people who don't like their jobs. If you have a mortgage to pay and children to feed, you can't simply leave your job tomorrow, however much you hate it. You have accepted commitments. Those commitments *are* your choices and they are the result of your free will. So while you may feel trapped in your job, remember that it's likely to be your choices that have put you there. Accepting this can make dealing with difficult situations easier. It can also make driving change easier, as it allows you to see what you can change, and what you can't.

Remember that no-one can interfere with your free will, unless you allow them to do so. Let's say you have a female friend who is engaged to a man who you believe is not good for her. He is a cheat, and you have evidence of this. But whenever you try to tell your friend that he's a cheat, and that she should leave, she refuses to believe you and refuses to leave. He is, she says, her true love. She is unable to see anything else. That's her choice, made with free will.

The more you try to persuade your friend that she should leave, the more uncomfortable you're likely to start feeling. This is because by trying to stop her from making choices, you're trying to interfere with her free will. This is an unnatural thing to do, and as difficult as it is, everyone must be left to make their own choices and learn their own lessons. These lessons are needed by our souls so our souls can grow. Some are difficult lessons to learn, but once learnt, they don't need to be repeated. If your friend is able to learn her lesson from her relationship, she won't ever have to experience a relationship of that kind again.

The soul longs for experience, and it will ask you for it. It wants you to make choices that allow it to have experiences. Everything is up to you. If you can open yourself to the idea that you can make choices, you stop allowing yourself to be a victim. No-one but you can control your life. You may feel that your choices don't matter or that your life is outside your control. If you do, it's because you've been conditioned to think this by influential people in your life. As you learn more about these particular subjects, their influence should drop away, as you learn how to make choices for yourself. And, as you make choices, you open yourself up to understanding your identity. You're able to hear your soul speak. If, at this point, you feel angry or frustrated, take a deep breath. Keep reading and learning. Our minds tend to reject what they don't understand. With greater understanding will come the ability to hear your soul. Your spirit guides and angels know this. They respect the fact you're in charge of your life and will never interfere with your free will. They exist to help, not to control. Only you can be in control. This knowledge that you're in control means there is nothing to fear from your guides. Let's now learn a little more about them.

Spiritual guidance

There is a beautiful line in the metaphysical text A Course in Miracles: 'If you knew who walks beside you on this way which you have chosen, fear would be impossible.'

When you trust and know that you're not alone you can live in peace with yourself and the world around you. Spiritual guidance can come to you via signs, synchronicities and warnings. You might overhear a conversation that tells you exactly what you need to know in that moment. Everything you need to know will come to you when the time is right. Relax into this knowledge and you'll understand that when something doesn't work out the way you want, it means there's something better on its way. Trust that you're where you need to be. When your soul makes its way into this physical world you tend to forget who you truly are. Restore communication with your soul and be open to guidance. Relax and *listen* to your soul. Your spirit guides and angels will teach you that you're your own best guide. They will encourage you to tune into your soul, where everything you need to know lies.

Signs and synchronicities

Butterflies

Whenever I see a butterfly, I know that I'm on the right path. If I feel discouraged or frustrated, the sight of a butterfly tells me to hold on, to keep going. The butterfly is one of the signs that my guides send me. It's also a sign of transformation and change. It brings me joy and helps me sweep past fearful thoughts. When I see a butterfly, I can hear the voice of my soul, and sense my guides are with me.

Sometimes, the butterfly comes to me as a picture on a postcard, or on a t-shirt print or a book cover. It might come in a TV show or a film. Recently, I was feeling frustrated and sad about something that didn't work out as I thought it would. Then a girl came walking along the road wearing a t-shirt with a butterfly on it. I knew that I would be okay. I felt supported and guided. I knew the spirit guides were there for me.

I'd like you to choose a symbol that has meaning for you, as butterflies do for me. This sign is your reminder that you're on the right path. Whenever you see it, you will know that you are being guided. This sign will remind you that you're not alone. When life is challenging, let this sign be a reminder that all will work out in your favour, and that important shifts may soon be heading your way.

Note: when you're guided to a sign and you start noticing it in your life, this demonstrates that you're open to the spiritual guidance that is your birthright. But, a word of warning: I often see people obsess about signs. They deliberately start searching for them, forcing themselves to see them, making the process unnatural.

For example, if a person's sign was a particular sequence of numbers, they keep checking their phone, waiting for the numbers to appear. Don't do this. It creates tension and anxiety. Trust that the guidance you need at any given moment will come to you. Your sign will appear when you relax and trust in the processes of life to take care of you.

My special guardian

For many years, my grandmother Emily has watched over me, since she has crossed over to the other side. She and I share a special sign, one that only the two of us know and understand. I can't tell you what this sign is, but I can tell you that sometimes I see it several times a day. When I feel discouraged or upset, I see it even more often. I know that she's guiding me and inspiring me to trust in my path. Sometimes, when I see this sign, I begin to laugh, or cry tears of joy. Our connection is strong and highly emotional. It's impossible to dismiss as coincidence.

Emily has been with me every day for over 14 years

now. She is a security that I can rely on completely. Do you have someone who could be your guide? Someone much-loved, but no longer physically here? Not everyone does, but if you do, get still and open up to receive their guidance. They may have decided to watch over you. Tell them that you're grateful for their presence and connection, for you are being watched over. They love you unconditionally and are here to help you and support you, even though they're not physically here. Just thinking about them is enough to create a connection.

Angels

We've all heard of angels, but we all perceive them differently. Some see them as biblical figures, some as symbols of protection, love and guidance. Many believe they are fictional, appearing only in fantasy stories and fairy tales. The world angel comes from Greek, Latin and Hebrew and it means messenger. In the Bible, angels bring the important messages to the world, such as the birth of the Jesus. They play an important role in religion, but they aren't limited to it. They've been an inspiration to artists, with many beautiful paintings and sculptures arising as a result. There are nine main choirs of angels: Seraphim, Cherubim, Thrones, Dominions, Virtues, Powers, Principalities, Archangels and Angels (the Guardian angels belong to this category). Each category has a different role to play, but there is no hierarchy between them. In this book I mention couple of the categories, because there are the angles I have experience of. Perhaps you too have already experienced the angels, or perhaps you haven't. Stay open-minded and read on.

Guardian angels

All souls, including yours, have a guardian angel. They are with us always, guiding, motivating and protecting. They are the gatekeepers to our souls. What do I mean by this? I believe that every soul has a guardian angel assigned to them when they incarnate into a physical body. This helps them through their journey on earth. They love us unconditionally for us every second of every day, for our entire lives. They are here, whether we choose to believe in them or not. They will never leave us and will always be with us. I learnt to feel and communicate with my guardian angel when I was very young, as taught by my grandma Emily. Every single morning and evening I say a prayer to my guardian angel and thank it for the protection it offers me.

If you're able to believe in your guardian angel, say thank you to it. Acknowledge the angel's presence and the love it offers you. This will allow you to connect with your angel and feel its guidance.

To create a connection with your angels, you can simply think of them. You can also say a prayer, to thank and acknowledge your angels. *Dear guardian angel, thank you for watching over me and guiding me every single day.*

You can ask questions about anything you would like help with. Remember that your angels won't interfere with your free will. They respect your free will. They will simply guide you with signs, synchronicities and warnings.

Archangels

I would also like to mention archangels. There are fifteen archangels: Metatron, Ariel, Chamuel, Uriel, Gabriel, Raphael, Michael, Sandalphon, Azrael, Jophiel, Haniel, Raziel, Raguel, Jeremiel and Zadkiel.

Each archangel has a different role, and we can call on each when we need a particular kind of guidance. I call upon Archangel Michael when I need protection and security. I call upon Archangel Raphael when I need healing.

All of the archangels are powerful healers, on whom you can call at any time. Many people worry when they call an angel or an archangel that they may be busy helping someone else, but there's no need. Angels and archangels are powerful, able to be in many places simultaneously. This sounds impossible, but it's only so in our three dimensional human reality.

How to contact archangels

I've chosen to use Archangel Michael as an example here, as he's the archangel I have the most experience with.

When you need help, close your eyes and take deep cleansing breaths until you feel calm and relaxed. Then, say this prayer: *'Archangel Michael, I call upon you now. Please surround me with your beautiful energy. Please shield me and protect me from anything negative I might have unintentionally attracted to me.'*

As you do this, visualise Archangel Michael shielding

you with his blue protective light. Trust and know that you're being helped as you say this prayer. Then, thank Archangel Michael by saying silently in your mind or out loud: *'Archangel Michael, thank you for your help and support.'* Take a couple of deep breaths and when you're ready, open your eyes and know that you're fully protected and that all is well.

Spirit Guides

Spirit Guides are spiritual helpers who have lived on earth in the past in human form. They might also have lived in other dimensions as beings of light, or perhaps in forms beyond our imagination. They have had many lifetimes and have gained much valuable experience of existence. They have then chosen to take on the role of guides for our souls on the earth. They exist in a different dimension and have frequencies different from ours. You may be able to tune into their frequency through meditation. We all have spirit guides and all of us can choose to get to know them, simply by being open to it. You may have more than one spirit guide working with you simultaneously. They may also enter and leave your life, depending on what you are currently working on, or going through. I've always felt the presence of my guides and I know they help me with what I do, when I ask. I know the guidance I need is always provided to me when I choose to listen. They don't interfere with my free will. They respect it. When I encounter challenges, I sometimes dismiss the signs the guides send my way. This happens when I'm more in my mind than aligned with my soul. We all do this, because our minds are so powerful. Our minds often take over and block the voices of our spiritual helpers. We can help prevent this by working to tune in to our souls through daily meditation.

Once we decide to make a connection with, and listen to our guides, the doorway to new adventures opens. The spiritual guidance is available to us all. We've forgotten how to access it because of the conditioning we've received. It's our birthright and natural inclination to communicate with spirit guides. You'll encounter many people who aren't yet ready to hear this. Be compassionate towards them. When the time is right, they'll open up, perhaps in this lifetime, perhaps in their next.

Spirit Guides of the highest truth

When you want help from your spirit guides, ask them for it. When I want to communicate with my guides, I invite them by saying: *'I call upon the spirit guides of the highest truth.'* This allows me to connect with only the purest guides, who will support, respect and love me unconditionally.

How to communicate with your Spirit Guides

If you're feeling confused about all you've learned in the last few pages, don't worry. You can learn to communicate with your spirit guides. Anyone can, if they are willing and able to listen. I don't mean you should listen for sounds, but that you should be open to signs from your guides through all of your senses. Your guides will use your aura, your energy field, to communicate with you. When you're able to sense your guides, you will sense their guidance without trying. The guidance often comes as a vision: a colour, a word, a picture, a feeling or a sound. You might feel that you're imagining this vision, but practise being open. Don't dismiss it. You don't have to do anything else.

Spirit Guides meditation

This meditation will allow you to develop your ability to communicate with your spirit guides.

Find a comfortable place where you won't be disturbed for at least five minutes. Take a deep breath, slowly in and slowly out. As you breathe in, imagine that you are inhaling a pure, white light. As you breathe out, imagine that you're exhaling thoughts and feelings that don't serve you, and that you've struggled to let go of. Repeat this five times, and then return your breath to its natural pace.

Now, ground yourself by imagining white light beaming through the soles of your feet, like roots anchoring you to the ground. These roots become stronger and you are safe and supported. Imagine a beam of white light coming from the top of your head, your crown chakra, connecting you to the rest of the universe. The connection grows stronger as you feel safer and more secure. You are connected to everything there is.

Shield yourself by imagining a white light surrounding you and protecting you. Know that nothing negative or disturbing can penetrate it.

Say: '*Spirit guides of the **highest truth**, I call upon you now. Please shield me, guide me and help me to see love and light in every being and every situation. Please help me to surrender and release any fears, worries and any thoughts of separation to a higher source, so they can be transformed back to love and light. I trust and know that I am safe and fully supported now.*'

If you have anything you want to ask or share with your guides, do it now. Notice your thoughts, feelings and visions. Don't judge or try to control them, simply acknowledge them.

Thank your guides for the support they have given you. Say '*Spirit guides of the highest truth, thank you so much for your assistance, help and support. I am very grateful for your unconditional love and continuous guidance on this journey called life. I love you and appreciate you.*'

Imagine pink light surrounding you. This is unconditional love. It is a shield, protecting you. Nothing can penetrate its strength unless you allow it to.

Breathe slowly and deeply. When you are ready, gently open your eyes. You are safe. You are secure. Your guides are always with you to help you. All you need to do is ask.

This is a general meditation you can practise to contact

your spirit guides. You can experiment and go deeper if you like. Use your own words and ask them anything you would like to know. You can ask for their name. You may not hear it straight away, but in time a sign may appear. It's also a good idea to keep a spirit guide diary. Use it to write down the guidance you receive so you don't forget what you've experienced. Record visions and intuitive messages. When you feel stuck you can refer back to your diary for insight and help. Your spirit guides may also appear in your dreams: note down anything you remember when they do.

The more you practise connecting with your guides, the more comfortable you'll become and the easier it will be. When I contact my spirit guides, I like to light a purple candle for protection and higher guidance. Have no expectations, be open and patient. Trust your intuition and the wisdom of your soul.

The universe is on your side

I once went on a holiday to Alaska, travelling for a couple of weeks. The nature and the energy of the place is incredible. When I returned to London, I was thrown by the time-zone change. I had a few days off before going to work, during which I was trying to deal with the time difference and get into my usual flow. This wasn't easy. If you're a traveller, you'll know how jet lag can impact you.

For a few days I was up all night, only falling asleep around 8 am. Then, came the day I had to go back to work. Working as cabin crew, I had to report for a trip to Singapore at 5 pm. This meant adding another eight hours to my jet lag. I was worried that I wouldn't be able to cope, and wished I could sleep an extra few hours. If I could have until 5 pm to sleep, rather than having to be at work then, I'd be okay.

I reluctantly set my alarm for 2 pm, and woke then, having fallen asleep at 8 am that morning. I had a couple of missed calls and a voicemail from work. My flight had been delayed, and I didn't have to report until 9.30 pm. Was it coincidence that this had happened when I so desperately needed more rest? I don't think so. I believe the universe, including spirit guides, angels and all the magical forces were on my side.

The universe is on your side too, if you choose to notice the synchronicities that happen all around you. When you choose to take the spiritual path, you choose to stop denying synchronicities as coincidences. You know that there are forces working to help you. This is a wonderful way to live, as you will no longer feel alone.

Freedom from fears and worries

Trusting and knowing you're not alone, allows you to become peaceful and happy. Your angels and spirit guides are always here for you and all you need to do is to ask for their assistance. My hope and belief is that this chapter will continue to help you reach for some new heights of the light. It will help you align to your own truth and realise how powerful you truly are. There is so much in your favour, Mystic Butterfly. You are a unique, magical and brave soul to be here in this time and space. You are guarded and taken care of, all day and every day that you exist.

CHAPTER SIX

COSMIC WONDER

Each of us is powerful, interesting and mysterious. Each of us is capable of creating beautiful things but also not-so-beautiful things. Sometimes our lives are wonderful, at other times challenging. We get lost, and then we find ourselves. I hope this book is already helping you to discover more and more about who you are and how you can enjoy your life.

In the last chapter, I talked about how there are powerful forces, spirits and angels, protecting and guiding us. When I first realised this, I felt quite haunted by it. Now, I see it as magical. Every time I make something happen in my life, I'm amazed by the way my soul and my physical self are able to co-operate, simply because I've allowed myself to find out who I truly am.

At this point, you may still feel sceptical. That's normal. Our minds often reject things that we don't understand until we're able to experience them. Keep reading, keep learning, and allow yourself the gift of discovery. With openness to new experiences and time to allow your brain to process them, you'll find new ways of thinking and doing.

Mystery, magic and miracle

Each of us connects to the rest of the world, and this connection gives us great power. There is an energy field around all of us that can make our dreams real. It responds to our thoughts, feelings and emotions. It reflects them back to us in material form. We create things and we attract things into our life.

The energy field responds to your vibration by giving you an experience of what you're currently feeling.

I call this field 'cosmic wonder'. A feeling begins with a thought and when a thought becomes a feeling, it creates a vibration. When you're happy, you feel that anything is possible. When you're sad, you feel uncomfortable, with a lump in your throat or a knot in your stomach. These feelings are strong, and can be created by a single, fleeting thought.

Once the feeling starts to vibrate, cosmic wonder responds. When you feel happy, and your vibration is happy, you feel that you deserve good things and positive experiences. When you feel sad, and your vibration is sad, you feel negativity and pain. You attract other things that vibrate at a similar frequency, and so one thought can become one feeling that attracts other feelings, and a circle of positivity or negativity is established.

Cosmic wonder simply reacts to your feelings. It doesn't know what you want or don't want. It only understands your vibration and responds to it.

Your soul is powerful, blessed with many abilities and unseen forces assisting it on its earthly journey, which may be yet to be discovered. If you're new to spirituality you may find it difficult to grasp the concept of such a power. This isn't surprising, given the way our world is generally organised. We're controlled by a few *chosen ones* who make decisions on our behalf. To make their own power secure, they make us believe that we're completely powerless and that we should always stick to the rules that they've created and we've accepted.

This gives us the nagging sense that something isn't right, even if we're not able to identify how or why. We have this feeling because our souls are telling us that there's something wrong. But, as humans with powerful minds, we tend to believe what the world tells us. Those who are brave enough to step out from the crowd and have a different point of view based on their own discoveries are often made a laughing stock. This is how we've been conditioned.

I don't want you to think that this makes you, or anyone else, a victim. Instead, think of it as an opportunity for awakening the ability to become open to new ideas. If you're open to ideas, invisible doors will start opening for you too. Choose to walk through these doors and you'll be shown a new perspective, one that allows you to search inside yourself, remembering incredible, long-forgotten secrets. Once you've opened yourself up, you'll find it impossible to go back to your old way of thinking.

All this knowledge is within you. Perhaps you've felt for some time that there's something not right about the world we live in. Maybe you feel that you didn't come here, to earth, just to struggle. You want to have a joyful experience, and you're right to want that. Now, your soul has directed you here, to this book, which may be a catalyst for change for you. Begin your own research, make up your own mind what and whom you wish to believe, but most importantly trust your own inner wisdom. If you can learn to co-create with the magical field that is cosmic wonder, you'll begin to live a life beyond your imagination.

How Cosmic Wonder works

Think about a radio. When you want to listen to BBC Radio 1, you set your radio to its frequency and you expect pop music to play. When you want to listen to Classic FM, you set your radio to its frequency and you expect classical music to play. If you want to listen to classical music, you would never set your radio to BBC Radio 1's frequency.

The same applies to you and your frequencies. You think a thought and you put a feeling underneath that thought. This creates a vibration sent to the cosmic wonder. The cosmic wonder then responds by sending you something which matches the frequency you sent out.

Imagine someone says 'I can eat anything and never put on weight!'

This is a powerful statement with a powerful secret behind it. The power is in the belief that underpins it. The person saying this has accepted within the whole level of their being that it's true. Cosmic wonder has no choice: it can only respond by matching this person's vibration, and by doing so, it makes sure they'll have the body they want.

Now imagine another person says 'I only have to eat one cake and I put on weight.' They eat that one cake, and they feel guilty and upset. A week later, as predicted, they weigh themselves and realise that they've gained a little weight again. Cosmic wonder had no choice but to give them this, not as a punishment, but because it was the only response possible matching that person's vibration. Cosmic wonder makes no value judgement. It simply responds to frequencies. It's just like your radio, which makes no judgement on your choice of music, but simply responds to the frequency you tune it to.

To have the life you want, you must believe in your ability to obtain it. When you do, the energy that flows around you will serve you in a positive way.

Speak to the cosmic wonder and it will speak to you

A few years ago I went on a trip to Thailand. I was still learning about the ways in which we connect and the universal laws that govern those connections. I had begun to understand that we're not separate from each other or the rest of the universe.

I decided that I would test the cosmic wonder, to see if it worked as I expected. I decided that I'd make sure that a cup of cappuccino came into my life that day. I set off to explore Bangkok's Grand Palace, feeling clear that the cappuccino would appear at some point. I released this desire into the cosmic wonder and then forgot about it as I got on with my day. I became absorbed into my tour, enjoyed the palace and met some wonderful new friends.

I got back to the hotel that evening, happy but a little tired. I decided to have dinner at the hotel restaurant rather than going out again. I'd forgotten all about the cappuccino. I ordered and ate some delicious Thai food, signed for my bill and then stayed at my table to listen to a beautiful piano performance. As an amateur musician, I have a strong love of classical music. While I was listening, the waiter came over to ask if I'd like anything else. I asked for a cappuccino.

An hour went by. I was still at the restaurant, and I'd drunk the cappuccino, but the bill hadn't arrived. Tired, I asked for the bill, again. The waiter, aware of how long I'd waited, said 'Don't worry, it's on us.' I told him I couldn't accept that, as I'd drunk the cappuccino. But he insisted that it was free, and so I thanked him and went to my room. As I got into bed, I realised I'd just had the cappuccino I'd decided I'd manifest that morning. I'd released the desire into the cosmic wonder, and hours later, it had returned in physical form.

It was much more than a cup of coffee. It was the start of a new, wonderful co-operation with the invisible energy field that surrounds us all. You can do this too. Learn to speak to the cosmic wonder, and it will speak back.

Telepathic thoughts

Have you ever found that when you think about someone, they call or text you? This has happened to most of us, more than once. We often label it as coincidence, but is it really? I believe not. We're all powerful spiritual beings, easily able to pick up on the vibrations that float around us. We see this with our connection to angels and spirit guides. Think of them, or call upon them, and they'll be there. As a divine soul, you are powerful.

Try this exercise. Think of a sequence of numbers, anything you like. Let's say you choose 1230. Focus on these numbers fully every day. For the next few days, start noticing how frequently you see them. You may find that every time you check your phone you see them. Perhaps you'll get couple of appointments at 12.30. Or your post will be delivered at 12.30. Take this as a sign of your unlimited power. Whatever you focus on always expands. Whatever you think about, you bring about.

Telepathic thoughts are natural. They confirm how strong your emotions and the vibrations behind them are. You may have noticed telepathy between you and another person. I've always noticed the telepathy between me and my sister. When we talk, we often tend to say the same things, at the same time, or I'll think of something and she'll say it just before I do.

Two powerful ways to stay on a high frequency

Gratitude

When you co-create with the cosmic wonder you should keep your vibrations as high as possible. One of the easiest ways to do this is to focus on what you're grateful for. Take a pen and paper and list everything you appreciate in your life. This exercise will help you shift your energy levels to higher frequencies. Write down everything you can think of. For example: *'I am grateful for my family, my health, the roof over my head, the food on my table, the eyes to see, the beautiful sunshine outside today, my dog, for friends I can rely on…'*

Being grateful for what you already have turns it into *enough*. We live in a world where most people value material things, such as cars and bank balances. And money does make life much easier, so of course we'll always need, and want it. But there are other things, that we often take for granted and fail to appreciate, which are more valuable, being precious and irreplaceable.

Stay in a state of gratitude as much as possible, rather than only when you're deliberately co-operating with the cosmic wonder and trying to manifest something. Gratitude not only shifts your vibration to a higher frequency, but it will also make you feel good. And when you're in this state of joy, anything is possible.

Positive affirmations

Affirmations are positive statements which can easily shift your vibration from negative to positive. They always help me to shift my perspective. When I find myself in a negative thought pattern, I try to change it using positive affirmations. I then change my frequency, feeling much better within moments.

Affirmations need to be positive, personal and in the present tense. For example: *'I believe in myself and I can do anything.'* Replace your negative self-talk with positive affirmations and you'll start shifting your perspective. This will help you co-create quicker with the cosmic wonder. Always write affirmations down, as this will make them feel more real and make them more memorable. Below is a list of my favourite affirmations, which you're more than welcome to use, or you can also create your own.

I am fully supported by the universe

Everywhere I go, I am completely safe

I am abundant in all areas of my life

Everything works out for me

Life is unfolding as it is supposed to

I trust the wisdom of my soul

I am healthy, beautiful, calm, confident, successful and happy

The art of co-operating with the cosmic wonder

We all have the ability to bring things we desire into our lives. You often hear people in spiritual circles talk about 'manifesting.' This is what manifesting is. It's our power to focus on our desire and make it real. If you can learn to focus on what you *really* want, feel good about it and of course, put some work and effort into it, you can bring it into your physical reality.

When you work with cosmic wonder, there are five steps you need to take:

- clarity
- belief
- feeling
- release
- action

Clarity:

What it is that you'd like to manifest? Be very clear about what you desire.

Don't say 'I'd like to go on a holiday.'

Be specific. Where would you like to go? When would you like to go? What airline would you like to fly with? What will your room look like? What's the view from your balcony? What's the hotel like? What adventures do you have while you're there?

Create these beautiful images in your mind and then write it all down. Don't be tempted to skip this step: it's vital.

Belief:

You must believe that your dream is possible. You must believe in your ability to make it happen. You must believe that you're worthy of your dream. If you don't believe, who will?

Feeling:

Cosmic wonder responds to your feelings, so you must feel that your dream will manifest. You should feel within the whole level of your being that your desire will come to you. Visualise and experience the feelings you will feel when your dream is manifested. You don't need to wait: feel these feelings now.

Think about the holiday. What would it feel like to be on the plane, on your way there? What is the plane like? Where are you sitting? How does that feel? Never forget that your imagination is endless, and you have the ability to create anything you like in your mind.

Release:

When we work to manifest something, we naturally hold on to it. We want it so much that it's difficult to let it go. Some things are easy to manifest, and others take time. Don't be discouraged or disappointed if your desire isn't met straight away. Know what you want and be prepared to get it. Release your worry about when it will happen, and trust the cosmic wonder. Relax and be open to any possibilities.

The cosmic wonder will do its work, so let it. Trust, don't obsess and know that what you want may arrive in a way that you don't expect.

Action:

When you want to accomplish something, you'll always need to take action. The universe will show you what action you need to take, so be guided by it. Notice signs and synchronicities around you. Follow them, as they can be your greatest guides. Taking action is not a final step, but one you should be taking every day as you're co-creating with the cosmic wonder.

Important points about manifesting

Start with small things

The cappuccino strengthened my belief. If you can start with small things too, the same will happen for you, and your co-operation with the cosmic wonder will become more and more natural and unthinking.

Trust

The universe is always on your side and wants you to enjoy your life. Be aware of that and know that you will always find your way. If something doesn't work as you want it to, trust that there's something else, something better and even more exciting on its way to you.

How to visualise

Take some deep breaths to centre yourself. Hold a vision of what you desire in your mind. Be clear about this. See it, feel it, allow your body to be filled by its emotions. Remember that the universe holds plenty for everyone. You're not asking for too much.

Are you clear and committed to your vision? Deepen these feelings. Know that the cosmic wonder is always working. Show it that your vision is important to you, and it will respond. Make your vision clear and powerful. This is the key to making it reality, for if you can't see it clearly, how can it be made real?

You may get flashes of images, places, feelings, thoughts or situations. Simply notice them, and smile. Trust, without worry or fear. Keep doing this, and you'll be speaking to the cosmic wonder. It will keep talking back to you, showing you what the universe has in store for you.

Now trust. Trust that what you want is on its way. Don't analyse or become anxious, simply have faith. If a negative or distracting thought comes to you, acknowledge it, and then clear it from your mind. Take a deep, cleansing breath and then see the negative thought fly away, like a dark cloud blown away by the wind.

Release your desire to the cosmic wonder, and know that the universe will bring it to you at the right time. Get on with your day, and when your desire comes to your mind, smile and know that it's on its way.

Then let it go again. It will happen when the time is right.

You attract what you are

The cosmic wonder responds to everything that vibrates from you. This starts with your thoughts. You are, naturally, the only thinker in your mind. You are the only person who can choose your thoughts. Decide to think good thoughts and you will create good feelings. Your feelings carry vibrations and these vibrations create your experience. There's so much in your favour in this universe. Allow the cosmic wonder to help you, not work against you. You have the power to choose what you would like to experience. Don't invest your precious energy on what you don't want, give it to what's important to you. It's that simple. Begin using your magical powers, Mystic Butterfly.

CHAPTER SEVEN

NATURE IS MY TEMPLE

Nature's beauty inspires, awakens and grounds me. When I begin to loose sight of myself, it brings me back. When I began my transformational journey, I quickly found that nature had the ability to be a hugely beneficial influence. Growing up, I was surrounded by nature all the time, hanging out in the woods almost every day. I had few friends, but in the natural world, that didn't matter. I could be myself, without pretence or feeling that I had to do things I didn't want to do. I would walk for hours with my father through meadows and forests, learning about trees, healing plants, mushrooms and animals.

As a young adult, I moved to London and lived fast. I stayed out late, slept little and indulged in alcohol and unhealthy food. But I couldn't live like that for long without acknowledging how unhappy it was making me. I took myself back to the woods here in England and rediscovered their healing powers. I was home and happy.

In this chapter, we'll explore the natural world and how it can heal our souls and our physical bodies. For this to happen, we need to be fully present, not simply walking through the forest, but being in it. The present is the only place where we can really live fully. We'll look too at the elements of nature: earth, fire, water and air. I'll give you some simple tools that you can use to work with to release the unwanted energy that holds you back from reaching your potential.

If you can, take the book somewhere beautiful and natural as you read this chapter.

Nature is filled with magic and secrets

In nature, we can see how powerfully life flows. Rivers fall unstoppably to the sea, seasons change each year and everything adjusts whenever and however it needs to. Animals don't wish the winter chill away. They simply accept it. They live in the now, never worrying about the future or the past. They go with the flow.

As the river flows downstream, it breaks through any natural resistance. If you've ever tried to build a dam with stones, you'll know how difficult it is. But what if someone builds a concrete wall across the river? It stops flowing and becomes muddy and dirty, but it keeps fighting to get through. If it is powerful enough, it will break through the wall and flow again, clear and beautiful. If it isn't powerful, it will stay still, becoming dirtier and more contaminated.

When we look at our lives, we can see how they often mimic this flow and resistance. Some of us build up strong walls that stop the natural flow of our lives. We try to control and manipulate so that everything happens as we want it to. We lose all faith in the natural flow. If something doesn't work as we want it to, we become frustrated, unable to believe that there may be something better on its way. If we could stay calm and be confident of change, instead of creating barriers, we'd be able to retain our power. Instead, like the river, we lose it, and allow ourselves to become trapped in a race we can't win.

Nature is a teacher. It gives us messages all the time, like the river. We just need to be open to reading them. If you're somewhere natural now, take a look around. What lessons could you learn from the grass, trees and fields that you see? Your soul will guide you. Your spiritual helpers are with you. Allow them to show you the way into the magic and secrets of nature, to explore and appreciate them. Be open to everything you see.

You don't need to travel deep into the countryside to do this. If you live in the centre of the city, find a park, however small, to enjoy. Any patch of green is enough.

The present moment, your real life

There is power in the present. Remember this, and stay in it. Constantly tripping into the future or dwelling in the past means we never get to experience the only thing that is really real: the now. Our intelligent minds give us the luxury of imagination. They allow us to be creative. But, without care, our minds can hobble us, keeping us stuck in the past or looking to the future and therefore unable to make the most of our lives.

If you're tempted to keep thinking of, and living in the past or the future, keep reminding yourself that they don't exist. Only the present exists. You can only create the life you want in the present. If you spend your time dwelling on past failures, or being fearful of future possibilities, you'll never be able to create change. The tools you need are always with you, but you will only ever be able to use them in the present.

In the last chapter, I introduced you to the energy field that surrounds you and responds to your thoughts and emotions. When you spend your time re-living your past, the field is confused and has no other option but to keep giving you similar experiences. It doesn't know what else to do, because it can only respond to your vibrations. I'd like you to make a decision, right now, to focus on what you really want. This allows you to take control of your life, directing your energy field to work for you, not against you. Be clear about your desire. Commit to it, and send it out with trust but without expectation. When the time is right, it will come.

What are you doing right now? You're reading these pages, but are you fully present as you do? Are you focused on what you read, or is your mind occasionally wandering? Don't worry if it is. It does for most of us, at least some of the time. We're taught to think ahead, to plan, to be ready for the next thing, all the time. Being present requires focus and training, but it is possible.

My mind is very imaginative and I often find myself thinking of the future, creating scenarios and worrying about what might happen next. I also often travel back in time, wondering what my life would be like if I'd done things differently in the past. But I always make sure I stop and ask myself 'where am I?' The answer is always 'in the present.' This is enough to keep me from straying too far from the present and losing my power as a result. I know that to lose the present is to lose my being.

If you find this difficult, remember that this is all about being able to enjoy life as much as possible. Whether you're drinking a coffee, reading a book or going to a dance class, you'll only truly enjoy what you're doing if you're able to lose yourself in it. Stop analysing a past you can't change. It has gone, and you can only make new choices.

The future traveller vs. the past traveller

For the next seven days, I'd like you to become very aware of your thoughts and where you direct them. Notice what you think, and whether you tend to think in the past, present or future. Every day, write down your thoughts and the emotions that come with them. Use as much detail as you can. At the end of the seven days, take a look back at your notes and see if there's a pattern. Do you tend to live in the present, past or future?

If you found your thoughts sit mainly in the past or future, you should now understand why you might be feeling stuck and frustrated. Now you know this, you can begin to focus on the present. This may not be easy, and you may find that you often fall back into old patterns. But stick with it, and you'll begin to see change.

Becoming present in nature

If you're struggling to live in the present, use nature to help you. Go somewhere natural. Ground yourself and breathe deeply. Allow yourself to become calm and feel peaceful. Watch the sky. Dance. Celebrate yourself. Remind yourself that nothing matters except the moment you're in. This is freedom, and you have it simply by staying in the present. It's the only place that real life exists.

The four sacred elements

The ancient Greeks believed that everything was comprised of four elements.

These four elements of nature are earth, fire, water and air. Together, they hold all the power of the world. Shamans, witches, healers and many spiritual teachers use them to heal themselves and others. Our bodies are made of them. They influence our personalities and behaviour. By connecting with the elements, we can learn about ourselves and everything that surrounds us.

I'll show you how working with the elements can clear your path of obstacles and enrich your human and spiritual journey. This is not just work for shamans. All of us can learn basic techniques which will rejuvenate our bodies, minds and souls.

Like everything else in the universe, the natural elements are connected. Air feeds fire, fire is extinguished by water, water is within the earth and the earth creates the air. They run together, connected.

Simple rituals using the nature elements

Earth (grounding and stability)

We all want to feel healthy, happy, safe and secure. We want to be taken care of, to experience stable relationships, free from drama. Without stability and safety, we live in fear and are ungrounded. In my twenties, I suffered from anxiety, was constantly afraid and worried about what others thought of me. I focused only on what could go wrong, not on what was going well.

It was when I discovered the healing powers of nature that I was able to ground myself. I found, sitting down under a tree, that I felt supported and connected to the earth. I felt calmer, my mind was clearer. I realised that rather than fight my feelings of anxiety, I should accept them and co-operate with them by working actively to ground myself. My experiences have led me to believe that many people who suffer from anxiety and panic attacks lack grounding from the earth element. Sometimes, people describe themselves as 'natural worriers'. I believe that natural worriers can feel much happier and freer if they are able to connect with the earth.

A ritual to try:

Find a healthy tree, one that appeals to you intuitively. Sit underneath it and feel your connection to the earth below. Feel it purifying your mind, body and soul. Know that it is healing you and rejuvenating you. Know, that you're safe and secure. Absorb the beauty of our earth through your senses.

Say: *'I trust in the process of life to take care of me.'*

Fire (purification and transformation)

Fire provides us with light, heat and smoke. Many people think of fire as dangerous and impulsive, but when we use it carefully, it can create transformation. It can be creative but also destructive. The most common symbols of fire are the sun and flames. The symbolic animal of fire is the phoenix, which is the legendary immortal beast and incarnation of The Burning God, Foiros, which rises again and again from its burning ashes. Its eternal flame can never be extinguished. It's also said that fire burns within our souls, moving us forward to work towards things we believe in.

Rituals to try:

To understand fire, head out into the sunlight. Feel the warm rays on your face. Wake up before sunrise and feel the power of the sun as it climbs in the sky. In the evening, watch it fall, transforming and purifying.

Use candles. I light them every day (except when I travel), including before and during every meditation class I teach. When you light a candle, you clear the space around it, so that negative energy falls away.

Incense sticks can have the same effect. I like to burn sage and holy wood (Palo Santo)

Say: *'I let go and dissolve anything which no longer serves me'*

Water (love, purity and the flow of life)

Water is cleansing and healing. It is soothing, fluid and pure. Water shows us how our life should flow. It nourishes us and all other living beings. When you wake up in the morning, you wash your face to feel awake and energised. Water is essential to our survival. When you are thirsty, it purifies you. Every time I have a glass of water, I visualise it cleansing me. Simply watching the flow of a river or the waves of the ocean has a cleansing and purifying effect on your mind, body and soul. Japanese researcher Dr Masaru Emoto believed that water is a blueprint of our reality and that our emotions change the physical structure of water. Dr Emoto carried out many experiments with water. For example, he spoke to water in both positive and negative ways and observed how it reacted to his words. He played music to water. He compared water in different glasses that had been exposed to different words. He took microscopic photographs of the glasses with incredible results. The water exposed to words such as love, gratitude and beauty formed stunning crystals. Water exposed to negative words such as hate or war became distorted.

Your body is made up of around 70% water. What thoughts and words are you telling yourself? Consider how your body and the water in it responds to these thoughts and emotions, and how they can change the way you physically feel. Don't judge yourself, just notice.

If your self-talk is more negative than positive, think about how to create changes.

Rituals to try:

Most of us feel drained and tired at least some of the time. It's often difficult to see what we can do about this, and many of us simply accept it, it's just how we live. But it doesn't have to be. When I feel like this, I find that taking a shower helps. Not simply a shower, but a spiritual shower. Turn on the water, and visualise the water washing away anything negative such as your fears and worries. As the water runs down your body, see it purifying your being. As the water runs away, down the plughole, see the negative energy running away with it, leaving you feeling calm and pure.

Go somewhere natural where there's a river or powerful stream. Watch how it flows. Simply watching it can have a strong purifying effect, bringing clarity to your mind. Breathe and relax.

You can also use the rain. Rain clears the air and cleanses the earth. Every time it rains, think of the earth being cleansed and freed from negativity.

Say: *'Life is unfolding as it should'*

Air (intuition and learning)

The air is all around us. Although it's invisible, it takes up space, it has volume and it exerts pressure. It is vital for our survival. We breathe air constantly, but we often take it for granted. We inhale and exhale naturally, yet if we weren't able to take another breath, we wouldn't last very long. Air can't be seen, but it can be felt. It represents everything that we can't see: our souls, our minds and other worlds. It opens our soul to freedom, and is a sign of liberation. Air can move anything we want to let go away from us.

Rituals to try:

Every morning, if I'm at home, I open my bedroom window and breathe deeply. I take a few breaths in through my nose and out through my mouth. I visualise the breaths cleansing and purifying my mind, body and soul. I can feel my auric field being cleansed too. I feel awake and energised.

On a windy day, I sometimes go outside for a few minutes and open my arms wide. I feel the wind blowing away my worries, fears and negative energy.

Say: *'With every deep, cleansing breath that I take, I feel more energised and empowered.'*

A thought to keep

Earth heals us, Fire transforms us, Water shapes us, Air moves us, Spirit guides us.

Where everything is pure

Whenever you go out into the natural world, take a deep breath in, and as you breathe out, let go of your worries. Know that nature is a natural healer. Allow yourself to be still and believe that all is well. If you feel overwhelmed and frustrated with life, as all of us do sometimes, simply tell yourself that *life is unfolding as it should*. I repeat this to myself every day as an affirmation to keep myself from worry.

Take a look at the trees you see around you. Every year, they change, in a cycle. They move with the flows of nature, unthinkingly. In spring, they bloom, in summer, they fruit. In the autumn, their colours become magical, and in winter, the leaves fall as they prepare for a restorative sleep and the spring blooms to come. Snow may fall and cover them for days or weeks. As the trees go through this cycle of seasons, these huge changes, they stand tall, firmly rooted, unflinching year after year.

Every season has its beauty. Sometimes, as during the blossoming of spring, the beauty is obvious. At others, such as in the bareness of winter, it's hidden, but still always there. The same is true of your life. Sometimes your life feels as if it's blossoming, at other times, it feels bare and you long for the blanket of winter to allow you to heal and grow again. Accept these cycles and learn to love them. They are part of nature and part of life.

Think about the animals. They don't worry as we do. They accept the flow of life, trusting the unknown path without worrying about the past or the future. They're engaged in the here and now. A deer may have been frightened by a hunter yesterday, but today, he is free and living life happily without fear. If another hunter comes, he will do whatever he needs to do at that moment.

Let the deer be your example. Visit the natural world and let it be your classroom. Observe, breathe in the air and allow it to heal you. Keep observing as the air clears your energy field, purifies your senses and your soul. Appreciate the freedom and the beauty of nature. Choose a tree and ground yourself within it, supported by it. Absorb its energy, allow it to flow. The elements of the earth show you how to live peacefully.

CHAPTER EIGHT

AND THE DARKNESS SHALL FADE AWAY

Our journey through life is not always smooth and easy. Things can get in our way when we want to make significant changes, or try something new. We'll make a decision to study a new course, lose weight or move abroad. This is exciting, and we feel ready for the challenge. We have energy and the belief that we'll make it happen. Then, we start to take action. We're still excited and still positive, until we face the first obstacle. Our self-belief is challenged, but it's still there. We keep trying, but then face more and larger obstacles. It starts to become very difficult to continue. We say things like:

Why did I decide to study this course? I'm too old.

I can't lose weight. I'll just have to accept my body as it is.

What's the point of moving abroad, it'll just be the same as home.

These thoughts become excuses, and we avoid meeting the goal we were so excited about just a short while before.

This happens when you haven't yet learned to communicate and co-operate with your soul. It's not easy to learn to do this. It takes work: daily commitment, practice and patience. It can be difficult, but it's very much worth it. In this chapter, you'll learn how to stay on the path in your own transformational journey, and how to keep on it, even when you want to step off.

The messenger of unhealed wounds

When we hit an obstacle and want to give up, it's fear that drives that desire. Unhealed wounds from our past create a belief that we're not good enough, and not able to continue. It's far easier to give up than to face the fear and continue.

As a child, I was very shy and full of fear. I didn't want to speak loudly for fear of being embarrassed. I didn't want to speak in class, for fear of being compared to others. I didn't want to tell my parents when I was bullied, for fear they would go to my school and tell the teacher. There were places I felt safe. At home, I loved to spend hours composing music, writing poems or pottering in the garden. I went on hikes with my dad. Despite my shyness, I felt happy on stage with my ballet school or singing as a soloist in church. I felt scared before every performance, but I could face my fear, as I felt I belonged on stage. I always performed well, and often surprised my audience. How could this shy little girl do so well?

I experienced a similar thing as a student pilot. I had been doing well on my course, and my first solo flight was coming up. I felt ready, I knew what to do, and I knew I was trained to deal with an emergency if I needed to. I was scared, but my instructor, Celine, had confidence in me. One day, we flew a couple of circuits in our little Cessna plane, and when we landed, Celine told the control tower that I would now be the captain.

'Are you sure I can do this?' I asked her.

'You're more than ready dear girl,' she replied. 'If you weren't, I wouldn't let you go. Enjoy!'

She unplugged her headset, shut the door and made her way back to the flying school. I started taxiing towards to the runway, my heart was pounding. It was time to prove myself. I made my final checks, and told the tower I was ready to depart. They cleared me for take-off, and I reached the beginning of the runway. Then, I surprised myself. Without hesitation, I applied full throttle and was in the air in seconds, flying alone. I felt amazing. I landed safely, applying all the techniques I had learned, and came in perfectly.

Everybody at the flying school congratulated me. The chief flying instructor who was watching me land said, 'Jana, that was a very stable approach and a beautiful landing. Well done!'

There have been challenges since. Longer solo flights, difficult navigation, cross country flying and the final skills test. I met every challenge and became a qualified pilot. I often felt scared, but I never gave up on my dream. Just as when I was on the stage dancing or singing as a child, I knew that what I was doing was my soul's calling, something I couldn't ignore.

I had to trust that I could become a pilot, because if I didn't, I wouldn't be able to do something that I felt I had to do. The fear was real, but it could be overcome. I chose to listen to my soul.

Stop haunting me now

Fear makes us want to turn back, and it makes us waste energy. It forces us into a negative spiral, where we feel there's no escape. When this happens to me, I have a tool I use to work with the fear. I don't try to push it away, but I co-operate with it. Your fear is part of you. See it as a shadow: part of you, something you can't take away.

I talk to my shadow, saying:

'I'm aware of your presence and I have no intention of pushing you away. Let's find a way to work through this together.'

When you try to push your shadow away, it will stay and haunt you. When you calmly accept it, it will calm down too. When you and your shadow are both calm, you can work towards achieving your goal. This might not seem easy, but it will be liberating. Try it, and see how much progress you can make.

This is also true of your spiritual journey and your work to communicate with your soul. Maybe you'll get discouraged. The meditations I've given you might not seem to work, as you struggle to quieten your mind. You'll try a spiritual shower, but won't feel the benefits. You might not feel your spirit guides. You might be confused and unsure if all of this is really for you. Don't panic. These feelings are natural and commonplace. Accept setbacks and fears, accept the shadows that follow you. Stepping out of your comfort zone can be difficult, and that's okay. Remember, as well, that your journey is your own, and shouldn't be compared to anyone else's. We all have different paths to walk.

Accept your fears, setbacks and shadows and work with them, not against them. They are part of your journey, part of your path. Just as a river flows downstream, without question or challenge, so you'll see your life flow. Each obstacle you come across is there to teach you, not to stop you. Each will help you connect with who you really are and that will be liberating.

What to do when you wander to the dark places

When you feel angry, upset, overwhelmed or worried, you tend to disconnect from your soul. You're unable to hear its voice, as it's drowned out by your feelings. When this happens, it's hard to shift back to your truth. Your energy gets low, you feel demotivated and every small setback feels like a huge problem. You want to get home, home to your soul, but you can't find the way.

When one thing goes 'wrong', it's easy to fall into the trap of seeing it as the first in a line of 'wrong' things.

I once had a first date with a person I'd liked for some time. We'd chatted online for a while and I felt we had a great connection. When we met in person, we felt very disconnected. The months of chatting we'd shared seemed like a lie. I'd had expectations of him and myself that I'd taken to the date. I'd turned up nervous and uncomfortable. Once I'd left, I knew we wouldn't see each other again. I blamed myself for this completely, thinking that I must have sent out bad vibes. The following day I woke up unhappy and upset, with a busy day ahead of me. I had errands to run, so I got in the car and started driving. As I did, everything seemed to be working against me.

Every traffic light was red. I drove into a multi-storey car park, and had to queue to get in. Every car in front of me had a problem of some kind, such as stalling or going the wrong way, delaying me further. When I had at last parked, I walked around the shops. Everyone was slow, uncoordinated and in the way. Every shop had a queue.

I usually feel as if I'm calm and approachable, but on that day I was selfish and inconsiderate. I wanted to get my own way, regardless of what anyone else around me was doing, or what difficulties they might be facing. I finished my shopping and headed for a coffee shop. They'd run out of the coconut milk I usually have in my chai latte. I began to feel angry, but then I realised it had to stop. I was creating the problems I was having myself, attracting people and situations that slowed me down. I sat and breathed. I imagined that I was breathing out my negative thoughts, and breathing in peaceful ones in their place. I visualised those thoughts with every breath. After five minutes of this conscious breathing, I was able to ask myself:

'What do I have to learn from this?'

The response came loud and clear, from the voice of my soul.

'You choose your thoughts. These thoughts create emotions, and you feel those emotions throughout your being. Choose your thoughts wisely. When something doesn't work out as you expected it would, know that better things will come. When you judge someone in your mind, look inward and ask yourself why you are choosing to make that judgement. Think not about them, but about yourself. If others seem to get in your way, consider that this may be a sign, a signal you need to read. Accept what is happening around you. Life has its natural flow and will provide you with the answers you seek, if you allow it.'

This message helped me then, and has done so ever since. It's part of the reason I decided to write this book. I believe that by knowing and working with the connection you have with your soul, you can make your life much easier. You're here to enjoy, not to struggle. When you find yourself in a dark place, it's often difficult to get out. But when you know and connect with your soul, you always can.

The Getting Home exercise:

Think of a time when you found yourself in a similar state to the one I was in, walking around that shopping centre. Now think about the next time this happens, as it will to most of us, at some time. When it does, take some deep, cleansing breaths. Tune inwards to yourself and your soul. Forgive yourself, your ugly thoughts and your unwise decisions. Remember that they've brought you to where you are now. Learn from them. Ask your soul what you have to learn from them.

You may find the answer to this comes easily, in a few minutes or hours. Or it may be the following day, week or month. Be open to messages and signs. They may come anywhere: on billboards, on TV, in conversation. Be vigilant and open to anything. Be gentle with yourself, because you're doing the best you can. Treat yourself well.

Your soul is always with you

Remember this, your soul is always with you and will never let you down. It will hold you when you need it. It will lift you when you need it. During a difficult time some years ago, my soul decided to write me a letter. I could feel my soul directing me to get a pen and paper, and start writing the letter. As I began to write, I could feel tears of joy falling. My soul had much to share with me, and I felt cleansed and liberated by the action of writing the things it shared. I will treasure the letter forever, and I've decided to share it with you.

Dear Jana

I love you so much and I am so proud of you. You are doing brilliantly as you walk your life's path and I am honoured to share this journey with you. I am so happy for everything we have done together and everything we have still to accomplish. I really believe in you. You have been through so much lately and I want to acknowledge that. All the struggles you have had are powerful lessons, the meaning of which will be revealed to you when the time is right. Remember I am always with you. We are in this together, we are one, and with our unity we can get through anything. I want you to know that you deserve the best. You are an amazing person and I want to remind you of that every day. Sometimes, I find it a little difficult to give you this reminder, and that's in the moments when your busy human mind overtakes my voice. Even though I may be screaming very loud, you sometimes have difficulty hearing me. Please know that in those challenging moments you can silence your inner critic by breathing deeply and being still. That way you will always be able to access my voice.

You are on the right path, and I know you will always do everything you can to do well in this world. I realise that our mission is big, and that sometimes you feel tired and discouraged. Please trust me. Don't be so hard on yourself, you're doing the best you can and you are doing very well.

You are amazing, Jana and I love you so much. You are perfect in every way and you are important, worthy and wise, even at times when you don't feel you are.

You don't have to feel stuck, because you're not stuck. You're not a victim, because together we are an infinite truth, beauty, love and peace all in one. Together we are more than capable of making this world a better place. This is why I've chosen to have this journey with you. You have done much work for us, and for that, I will always be grateful. Many others would have given up. You always persevere and never take your calling for granted. You've always known that you have a higher purpose.

We have much work to do, and I can't do it alone. I can only work through you, so I thank you for being strong for me. We're here to create great things, and I know we can. I'm so glad that I've chosen to be part of your life, in this time and space.

Let's get to work again. The world is waiting for us and the healing we can provide. I trust you, and know that together we will support our united existence here on earth, and one day we'll look back, proud of our work, and the incredible shifts we've made in the world and the entire universe.

Thank you so much for what you've done so far. I love you more than anything.

Always with you

Your Soul.

This is the letter my soul channelled to me. As you learn to communicate with your soul through this book, listen to what it wants to share. Be still, breathe and notice the moments of stillness and revelations your soul offers you. These may be brief visions, or premonitions or simple knowings. Pay attention to them and don't take them for granted.

You can also write a letter to your soul expressing your appreciation of it, or you may find your soul writes a letter to you, as mine did. It will deepen the connection between the two of you, between your physical and your spiritual side. Allow this process to come to you naturally.

Stay pure and keep your vibration high

It's vital that you keep your energy field clear and protected, as much as you can. This is what your soul longs for, because it will make it feel cleansed and purified. There is much love and light in our world, but there is also darkness. This darkness is where low energy, negative people and bad news lies. I say this not to scare you, but to make you aware. These things can affect our energy field, our aura.

But remember this, there are many powerful techniques we can use to protect ourselves against bad energy. As part of my training and development as a healer, I've learnt many of these techniques. This knowledge has been a gift. In spiritual language, we call it psychic protection. When you include some of these techniques in your daily life, as rituals, you'll see benefits, of that I am sure. I use them almost daily, any time I feel ungrounded or out of alignment with the world around me. Use them in the morning to give you power as you go about your day. Use them in the evening to give you undisturbed, peaceful sleep.

White light

Visualise a pure, sparkling white light around your whole being. Know that nothing negative or disturbing can penetrate through this light without your permission. It's a shield of protective energy. Anything negative that reaches it will be sent upwards and transformed into positive energy.

Mirror work

Visualise four long mirrors around you. One stands in front of you, one behind you, one on your left, one on your right. They are turned away from you, so that they can reflect negative energy away from you. Trust that the mirrors will do their job. Visualise the energy they reflect being transformed into the purest white light, so that it cannot harm any other being, either physical or spiritual.

Angels

Visualise beautiful angels around you, guarding and protecting you. When you're at home, trust that there are angels behind each door and each window. Be reassured that they are guarding you through the night, making sure you have a peaceful night's sleep, every night.

Aura cleansing

Take a few deep breaths and draw your attention inward to your soul. Visualise an invisible comb in your hand. When you are ready, brush your aura from the top of your head, all the way down as far as is comfortable, just as you would comb your hair. As you do this, trust that you are releasing negative energy from your aura. When you finish, visualise all the negative energy being transformed back to positive, so it cannot harm any other being.

Cleansing with sage and Palo Santo (Holy Wood)

You can use sage and Palo Santo to cleanse your home. You can buy these at any spiritual or new age shop, or online. Take them, and light them (the packet will tell you how). Use their smoke in every corner. Carry the smoke over yourself, to cleanse your energy field and your chakras. You and your home will feel balanced and purified immediately.

A thought to keep

When you find yourself in a dark place, don't be too hard on yourself. Understand that this is a detour, and detours are part of your journey. Instead of judging yourself, accept yourself. Learn the lesson that the detour has to teach you. Know you always do the best you can, with the knowledge and understanding you have at the time. Life is unfolding as it should.

CHAPTER NINE

COSMIC ONENESS

When I was seventeen years old I fell in love with a boy from our village. I idolised him. Every time I saw him, my heart would pound. I knew he didn't feel the same, but I also intuitively knew that one day, he'd notice me. We would be together. And it happened, but it wasn't as I hoped it would be.

He didn't accept me for who I was. He was embarrassed to be seen with me in public, saying it would be better if I was from a different village. Everyone in our village knew each other well and would talk, he said.

I was naïve, young and needy. I knew he didn't love me as I loved him, but I wanted to stay with him anyway. I believed inside, that I wasn't good enough, and his behaviour reflected back that belief. My insecurities flourished.

The relationship lasted only a few months before he left, but I didn't stop loving him for years. I met him again when I was twenty-three and living in London. He lived in Europe, and as I was cabin crew, I could visit him easily. I would meet him regularly, and everything felt different. I had, I felt, found my way back to my true love. And, he had changed. He apologised for the way he'd behaved when we were younger, and for embarrassing me.

Our reconnection happened during the time I was experiencing my big crisis, following my panic attack on the plane. I needed someone to run to, and so I ran to him. I felt safe with him, and despite everything that had gone before, he was able to provide the light I needed.

A catalyst for change

I was learning much about myself during this time, and I realised that to do that, I had to end the relationship. It was a tough breakup, and he was left devastated. I told him that I had to go, that I had somewhere else I needed to be. While this was hard, I knew it was the right thing to do. I had learned to put myself first, something I'd never been able to do before.

My journey to self-acceptance was just beginning. I'm still on that journey, working to discard old energies that no longer work for me. But I've come a long way, and one of the most important things I've realised is that *nobody is better than anyone else*. We place labels on ourselves, but they don't define us. We are all souls and that's our true nature. It took me a long time to come to this realisation, and for a long time, the belief that I was not good enough destroyed me inside. But status, money, class, education and career count for nothing, so all that worry and destruction was unfounded.

The creation of labels for each other has become a habit of humanity. When we meet a new person, we ask them what they do for a living, because when we know that, we can categorise them (well some of us do). We then know whether they're someone we want to accept, or not. But these labels, these categories, mean nothing. I learned this the hard way, after many years of pretending to be someone I wasn't. I believed I was a nobody, and so I had to pretend in order to stand a chance. I couldn't be myself, because that made me too vulnerable.

Pretending didn't feel good. It meant that I denied my truth, which hurt my soul. My relationship with my ex-boyfriend, and the challenges and changes it brought me, helped me to understand this. I'm grateful for that experience, as difficult as it was. It did much to help me accept myself and be proud of who I am. I used to think I wasn't good enough. Now, I know I'm good enough and I believe in myself, and the world reflects that back to me. I feel that my ex-boyfriend's soul and mine had a sacred contract together, and that we each helped the other learn things we couldn't otherwise have learned. Today, he's married with a family, happy to be the person he came here to be, and I'm genuinely happy for him.

In the rest of this chapter, we're going to explore unity and cosmic oneness. This is all about our truth and the importance of valuing that truth, rather than a label. When you value your truth, you can live an authentic life. When you live an authentic life, you're able to shine a light around the world. The only boundaries are those that you create for yourself through fear.

This is not just about individuals, but about all of us as a collective. We're all connected, but our false beliefs mean that we don't always realise it. Our beliefs sometimes damage us. I believe we must start again and work together to treat our world with respect and care. If we can dissolve the darkness, a better future lies ahead.

The world of illusion

Each of us creates our own reality, and so each of us perceives the world differently. Albert Einstein told us that time and space are illusions of our consciousness. In our world, days have 24 hours and years have 365 days, when they're not leap years. Seasons change and the weather changes. The sun rises and sets. But, if we were somewhere else in the universe, somewhere outside of our world, we would maybe never see the sun rise or set, as it would be visible all the time or not at all. It's all about our perception. Another example could be looking at the colour blue. Let's say we are looking at this colour and we both agree it's blue. But the truth is, you may have a completely different perception of what blue means to you, compared with mine, even though we've agreed the colour is blue.

Now, let's look at it from a soul's perspective.

Your soul perceives your reality differently from the way your human mind does. It sees no obstacles for you. Instead, it sees possibilities. It trusts spiritual guidance. It knows that life doesn't end when the body dies. It wants to experience everything that you do, especially the physical things.

The soul knows a lot, even though it hasn't yet experienced everything on a physical level, or any other level beyond our human imagination. This may seem like a nonsensical statement, but as you get to know your soul better, it will begin to make sense to you, as it has to me now.

Are you open to see the world from more than your own perspective? To be able to do so liberates you from the ties the world has placed on you. Your human, physical perspective leads you to want to be grounded and supported at all times. But your soul's perspective is different. It is the Mystic Butterfly, ready to experience everything the universe has and is, as fully as possible. You can keep both your physical self and your soul happy. There is no need to choose.

You've already learned that you have the power and ability to make choices. You have a free will that no-one can take from you, however hard they try. This means that you have the ability to create your own truth, one that works for you and your soul. It's time to move away from the illusion of darkness and live the life you deserve to live. Incredible lives come to real people, not just characters in films and books. Choose the life you want.

The labels are not oneness

In chapter two, I talked about how beliefs are formed, and how we learn to accept labels for ourselves as soon as we're born. These labels are very difficult to escape from, but it's important to realise that they're not who we are. They don't have to define us or our worth as people. One person might have multiple qualifications while another is unskilled. One might own a house in London and a holiday home in France, while another struggles to pay rent on a studio flat. One might have parents with well-paid jobs and inherited money, while another grew up with parents who struggled to pay the bills. All of these people are equal. Understanding this leads to cosmic oneness.

My own parents, both very creative and artistic, worked hard in low paid jobs to finance my sister's and my education and give us a better future. I was lucky, even though I wasn't born into money. But not everyone is born with the driven, motivated parents like mine. Some highly talented people, who could achieve multiple qualifications and glittering careers with the right support, lack any support. They struggle all their lives because they choose to accept that they were born to struggle.

Creating a shift in our consciousness

No person is worth more or less than another. If we, as one earth, accepted this truth we would all be able to be so much more. Our ways are outdated and wrong, both for individuals and for all of us as a whole. Let's rise up for happiness, against the dark forces that influence us. Let's start from a place of love and hope. If we can do that, we will be better prepared for a life of love and truth. Future souls will come to this earth and know what it means to live in paradise. I believe we're capable of this, but I know that to do it, we must *choose* to do it.

Letting go of old stories

In order to live at peace, we must be able to let go of stories that damage us. We have to be willing to see ourselves differently. We must be honest with ourselves about who we are. And we must be willing to share the knowledge we gain with others, to inspire and motivate them to let go of their own damaging stories. Be a living example of authenticity, and others will learn from you.

I have developed exercises and rituals that can help you do all of this. Let go of your old self and open your mind to the light.

Rewriting your story: an exercise

You may not have realised that you're doing it, but the chances are that you've been telling yourself a story all of your life. It may be that the story you've been telling yourself is inspiring and motivating. It may be that your story has been holding you back and causing you to struggle.

For example, your story until now might have been:

'I've suffered a lot in my life, I've felt in pain most days, and I've often asked what I could have done to deserve this kind of life.'

You could rewrite this story as:

'I've been through many challenges, but I've always coped well. These challenges have been painful, but they've allowed me to become who I am today.'

Think for a moment about what stories you tell about your own life. Now, think which of these stories is one that you'd like to change. Can you rewrite it using positive language? Doing this will shift your energy and help you achieve the life you want.

Dissolving resentment

Perhaps there are, or were, people in your life who've treated you badly. Perhaps you feel upset about world events or politics. Perhaps you're angry and frustrated with people in general and can't identify why. I understand all this, because I've felt the same way myself. But I've learned to let go of negative feelings using meditation. Try the meditation below to help you do this, too.

Cord cutting meditation

Find a comfortable place where you won't be disturbed. Take a few deep breaths until you feel calm and centred. Then, visualise a person or situation you resent. Visualise a cord of energy between you and this person/situation. Think about the cord. Where is it? What colour is it? How does it make you feel? Identify which part of your body feels most uncomfortable when you think about this. Now, I'd like you to invite Archangel Michael to help you.

As you may remember from the Mysterious World chapter, Archangel Michael is the angel of protection and security. His name means 'He Who is Like God'.

He has a golden sword he can use to help you cut the cord. Ask for his help, either out loud or silently, whatever you feel most comfortable with.

'Archangel Michael, thank you for helping me to cut this cord. I know that the resentment I hold doesn't serve me and I'm ready to let it go. I am ready to start living a happier, more fulfilled life.'

Then, visualise Archangel Michael cutting the cord, with one swift cut. See the cord fall to the ground and dissolve. You may feel relief immediately, or you may find this takes some time. Be patient and trust that the job is done and your resentment will dissolve. Thank the Archangel Michael for his help.

You can repeat this as many times as you like or need, either for the same situation, or different ones.

Beauty and authenticity

In my teens and twenties, I didn't accept myself as I was, and as a consequence, spent many years trying to be someone else. I used fantasy in a damaging way, making up stories in my fearful mind about who I should be, telling others that I had successful, happy life. In reality, I was miserable, suffering internally and acting from a place of fear and shame. I was untruthful because I didn't think my truth would be accepted. When I looked at myself, I could see only flaws, not my beauty, wisdom or intelligence. I believed I was worthless, while others were better than me, by virtue of their social class, nationality or education.

This was a painful way of living which contributed to an emotional breakdown. But I wouldn't change one day of those difficult years. They are what allowed me to find my true self, and for that, I'll always be thankful. I've forgiven myself the pain I caused myself, and the silly lies I told others when I was struggling deeply.

Today, I love and accept myself entirely. Every day that passes, I find my desire for self-acceptance grows. Self-acceptance is an incredible gift, one that I'd like you to give to yourself. Bring your uniqueness out into the world, and it will be a gift for all of us, too. It might not be easy to do this. We're all constantly told how to act and how to present ourselves. It's easy to believe that you should follow the crowd, and that if you don't, you'll fail. This belief can create huge pressure. We were born to face this challenge by bringing our true self to the surface, our authenticity being a powerful example to all around us. Release the pressure you feel by reminding yourself that you're good enough as you are, with nothing to prove to anyone.

I don't mean to suggest that you can't improve and grow. You can do this, while still accepting yourself as you are. But I believe that you must always work to align yourself with your own truth. That way, you're able to feel content with life and its ebbs and flows. You'll be in a much better position to strive for growth than if you're trying to be someone you're not, and dealing with the struggles that brings. When you're aligned with your truth, you have the space you need to be creative and adventurous, anchored by the knowledge that you have no need to pretend.

When I allow myself to be who I am, I'm empowered. I know that I came to this earth to be me, to be Jana. I love flying aeroplanes and listening to classical music, and sometimes hip-hop. I'm sensitive, and have interests some describe as 'quirky'. I'm in love with nature and everything mystical. These things are neither inherently good nor bad, but they're all me, and I'm proud of me. When, instead of being who I really am, I begin to compare myself with others and mirror their behaviour, I feel very different. Unhappy and uncomfortable and unable to live life to its fullest.

Think about yourself. What makes you who you are? What is it about you that you should be proud of? Allow yourself to value those things. They're valuable because they're you. One of my wonderful teachers and a dear friend of mine Maxine, once said to me:

Jana, the true power of yourself lies in your vulnerability. Get more in touch with that part of your being.'

I know that when I feel content and aligned with my own truth, others can easily pick up on it, as well as when I'm not being fully myself. It does take courage to be yourself, but it's the most important thing you can do for yourself. Accepting your flaws and celebrating your strengths, allows you to be free from worry and fear of yourself. I want you to make a decision now, to forgive yourself for pretending to be someone you're not, and to live your truth, every day.

The benefits of living your truth

- It empowers you
- It liberates you
- You will feel at peace
- You will find your life's purpose

Sacred Earth and the collective consciousness

To fully understand cosmic oneness is to honour the space we live in: the earth. I've decided to dedicate the next few pages of this chapter to earth, our sacred mother, with an intention to create a shift in our collective consciousness.

I feel honoured and grateful to have been born now, in this time and space, on this beautiful blue planet. I am so proud that I can call earth my home. She is our mother and protector. She has welcomed us humans to occupy her space and has always been there for us, giving us all that we need for survival. Like any other being, she longs to be loved and cared for. She wants to be protected. I believe we all have a duty to provide that love and protection.

Many people are unappreciative of what the earth has provided for us. Many attack and destroy earth, because they don't stop to think about how much she has done for us. They take her for granted, and I believe this causes her pain. I think we can all learn to live peacefully together, but to do this, we must make a conscious choice.

If we all decided today to live our lives in harmony, how much do you think our lives would change? I believe we'd see a significant and rapid shift in our human experience. This would happen because of the shift in our collective vibration that would occur, allowing us all to attract healing and freedom. National borders, racism and separation would dissipate and we would all live in truth.

Awakening

None of what I have said in this chapter is intended to create guilt within you. It is intended to help the part of you that has been sleeping to wake up. With this awakening you'll be able to see things that you've never been able to see before. The detail you've missed will become clear. You'll understand the work that all of us must do to make our world beautiful.

I challenge you to take responsibility for your own life, to be the light leading the way so that others may be guided by you. This is our home, and it is ours to look after. You are here to be a human, for just a short while. Make the most of that time, live consciously and make a difference. If you feel insignificant, or as if you can't make a difference, put that feeling aside. I know that you're capable of creating, inventing and making a difference, if you let your soul guide you.

An exercise in appreciation

Take a moment to go outside and breathe. Look around you. Feel how privileged you are to experience being alive, right now, at this time and in this space. Feel the ground beneath your feet, honour the air you breathe. Use your senses to fully experience being a human. Appreciate the freedom you have to explore your home on earth. Commit to treating the earth well. Acknowledge your role to play as part of a collective whole, a gathering of people who were once separated and can now come together. Each of us can do our part to create a shift in our collective consciousness. Give thought as to what that means for you.

A state of oneness

Relax and connect to your truth and your soul. Be full of love, gratitude and appreciation, and know that we're all united. None of us is less or more than anyone else. All of us are equal, here for the same reason: to enrich our collective existence. Your purpose in life is not just about you and your desires, but about all of us.

In the next and final chapter, you'll learn how to set about the adventure of finding your purpose. I hope you'll finish this book knowing how to look beyond labels and lies, do good and express truth everywhere you go. You'll be ready to love yourself and accept others. You'll be capable of spreading light and positive vibrations wherever you go. Our planet is sacred, and we're fortunate to be on it. Every positive action we take sends out a message to the cosmic wonder that we're ready to experience a shift.

To end this chapter, I've written a poem for Mother Earth, to pay respect and show her my appreciation. Perhaps you'd like to take this poem with you to your meditation space or spiritual circles, or just when you go out into the natural world. Read it and know that she will hear it and appreciate it.

Love to the earth

The beauty of planet Earth always amazes me,
and I am so grateful for her love, for her wisdom
and everything she has ever done for me.

There is something so unique and wonderful
about our home, our mother, our protector...
so let's honour her by living in peace, harmony
and surrender...

Surrender our worries, our fears and everything
which no longer serves us...
and that way clear the space, the energy field,
so she can breathe freely and smile at her children.

The beauty of planet Earth awakens us to our truth...
living our lives in peace and harmony
and in complete trust that all is good.

So, not just for today, but always... let's be thankful,
honouring our home, our earthly plane, and thanking her

for her love and her uniqueness in this universe
by being grateful.

Imagine…

Imagine Earth restored to her true beauty, and imagine living here in peace and unity. Imagine contributing to this awakening by being your authentic self. Imagine love being our universal language. You *are* powerful. The shift we all long for starts with you.

CHAPTER TEN

ENCHANTED WANDERLAND

As a child, I was often told, and still am, that I live in a fantasy world. As a child, this upset me, as it was proof that I was strange and different. As an adult, I take it as a compliment. It encourages me. I have realised that all of us live in a fantasy world, even the most practical-seeming of people, because all of us create our own reality. We can make this reality as mysterious, or not, as we like. Our lives are our own to shape as we choose.

In my life, I daydream, visualise and create. I create a reality that works for me. There are many spiritual teachings, traditions and views out there. Some of them work for me, and I follow them. Others, I find I don't agree with. I chose those that resonate with me, reflecting my life and my own experiences. You can do this too.

Be unapologetic about your choices. We all have a self, different to any other self. Own and accept yourself as you are, and be proud to make choices and decisions through your fantasies. Have the experiences that you want to have, not those someone else wants you to have.

The journey I've taken myself on has led me to colourful places filled with magic and mystery.

Discovering these places has helped me align with my soul by finding my true life's purpose. Now, I know that my life's purpose is to share my soul's wisdom, and to inspire others to access the wisdom of their own souls. When you let go of your old story and tune in to your true self, you will find the space you need to create change. This will lead you to your life's purpose. I can't tell you what this purpose is, but I can guide you closer to it.

Everyone has a purpose

Many people feel lost and confused about what they came to earth to do. They feel stuck and believe themselves to be victims. Their early conditioning means they've taken on damaging beliefs from a very young age.

Perhaps this sounds familiar. If it does, I hope you've begun the process of dissolving those damaging beliefs as discussed earlier in this book. Once you've dealt with one belief you'll find it easier to sweep away the others too. This is a beautiful, liberating task to take on. It will allow you to see opportunities and possibilities rather than obstacles. We all want to do great things in life, to be happy and enjoy life to the full. But we get stuck, confused, discouraged and doubtful. We think it's for others to shine, not us. We think others are more intelligent, better qualified or generally more competent than we are.

This isn't true. All of us are capable of doing whatever we choose, whatever brings us joy and fulfilment. We get excited about something when it's the thing our soul longs for. The excitement is a call from our soul, one that needs to be answered.

Your soul has a purpose. This purpose can often be found hidden in your talents, the things you love doing that bring joy to your soul, the things that light you up. You have chosen to fulfil your own mission. No-one else can do it for you. Your gifts are needed, and you came here to shine. It's time to enjoy this adventure, not struggle through it.

Like me, you have much work to do here on earth, but if you allow yourself to stay in the victim zone, you won't be able to do it. Whatever has gone before is done. Like me, you don't have time to feel sorry for yourself and your old story. That's done – now is the time to take responsibility for change.

Discovering your purpose

You might be asking yourself: *'do I have a purpose here? How can I find it?'* The answers to those questions lie within you. When I was a child I was very curious about life like many children are. I often kept asking myself: *'why am I here? What is the meaning of this journey?'* Many similar questions were often floating across my mind. You may think it's a bit deep for a child to think this way. To me, it wasn't. I knew from an early age that I came here to do something great and there's more to life than what I could see. There were obstacles, difficulties with other people's views, which were saying the opposite. But deep down, I just knew the shift would happen.

As a little girl, I often had visions of seeing myself on a stage with a microphone, either singing or giving a speech. When I experienced these visions, I then realised that one day, I didn't know when or how, I would share what I loved with the world. When this happened, it would feel right, because I'd know that this was what I'd come to do. When I got older, overcame some difficulties, and aligned with the voice of my soul, things got so much easier. I learnt to listen and pay attention to the signs. That's how I discovered my purpose. I can see very clearly now that all the things I've ever done and experienced fitted together so nicely, and led me to my life's purpose and to the story I'm still writing. It started out as confusion, but the indications were there. Listening *slowly* and by being patient, I couldn't ignore the revelation and mission which one day presented itself to me. The call was undeniable and it felt right. Tears of joy started pouring down my face, and a sense of peace and liberation took over my entire being. I realised:

I love inspiring others and I love talking about topics I care about and strongly believe in. I can talk for hours about spirituality, creativity, dreams, mystery and about flying and adventuring. It brings so much joy to my soul when people get inspired by these conversations. This is one of the reasons I believe my purpose in life is inspiring others and helping them to find their true gifts, so they can share them with the world.

The adventure I've started also brings me much joy and excitement, even though it can seem difficult at times. Ever since I've learnt to listen to the voice of my soul, the answers to any kind of questions come more naturally to me. I've discovered my life's purpose, and my soul and the universe are continually showing me which way to go. I'm willingly following this call and it feels very natural to do so. You and your soul also have a purpose here on earth and it's your responsibility to find it and share it with the world.

Exercise:

Get a pen and paper and find a quiet place where you're not going to be disturbed for a few minutes. Close your eyes for a moment and take a few deep breaths. Put any worries of the day aside for a few moments. You can come back to them later if you choose to. When you feel relaxed, open your eyes and ask yourself these questions:

- What brings me joy?

- What talents do I have?

- What do I love doing so much that I forget about the time?

- What activities did I like as a child?

- What do I like to do, that I'd do it, even if I didn't get paid for it?

Write your answers down. In the answers to these questions will be hidden your own unique life's purpose. You can also meditate and ask your guardian angels or spirit guides to give you signs. They'll be more than happy to assist. Remember, you're a soul with a free will and all you need to do is ask, then guidance will be given to you. The next step will be revealed to you.

Your adventure matters to us all

You are important and you are worthy because you're here. That's enough to know. As you're discovering your life's purpose, it's also your responsibility to share the gifts you possess and uncover with the world. That way, the earth and the entire universe can experience some major shifts in collective consciousness.

The veil is lifting

You know now that you're powerful and capable of creating a significant impact on the collective consciousness of the world. The veil to the unknown is now lifting and you're able to align with your true identity. Being a powerful, infinite being having a temporary human experience, you can accomplish anything you choose to, to make your life an *Enchanted Wanderland*.

If you want to take full advantage of your power, I suggest you use the following three techniques daily. Collectively, they'll have a radical impact on the earth and the universe. Use them, and we'll all benefit. All you need is an open mind and a willingness to make the world a better place. Choose to keep your vibration high, and you'll be making *your* contribution to great shifts in the world. The scale of your power and your ability to contribute to the healing of all of us is phenomenal. Never believe that you're too insignificant to make a difference.

Your radical impact on the planet and the entire universe

Realise that each new day is a miracle

When you wake each morning, use your waking as an opportunity to shift your energy level upwards. Remind yourself that it's a gift to be alive and breathing. You have a reason for celebration. Remember, some people didn't wake up this morning and you did.

Express gratitude for your life every morning, because each morning is a new chance to continue your adventure and a chance to be better than you were yesterday. Each day, you can decide to correct your mistakes, apologise, forgive or change your mind. You can choose to be kind to others, and to present your talents to the world. Each day, you're new and can start over, simply by deciding to do so. Treat your life as something to celebrate, not to rush painfully through. Trust that you're safe and secure, supported by the higher power that surrounds you. Every day is a miracle.

Accept that what has happened served its purpose

If you can accept that difficult past events have served their purpose, you will start to heal. In turn, your healing will contribute to improvements in our collective consciousness. Accepting
that something can't be changed but that it can be a lesson which has served its purpose brings peace and calm to the soul. Perhaps you feel you can't accept the past. You've had experiences or done things that you wish you could change. Maybe you've been hurt, and find it difficult to let go of that hurt. Perhaps you find yourself replaying scenarios in your mind.

All of this is understandable. You have the right to feel these feelings. Not allowing yourself to feel them would be to live a lie, and that would be a waste of our time and energy.

Change the way you think about unpleasant emotions. See them as signs that something needs to be healed, transformed or released. Feel them, but do so knowing that blessings will come out of those experiences. Acceptance will provide relief for your soul. Your mind may want to fight, but your soul wants to learn, let go and grow. It may not be obvious yet what the lesson is, but it will always be revealed eventually.

I wouldn't change a day of my dark days. They taught me so much about myself. Many blessings and redirections came out of them. They have made me stronger. They are part of the person I am today, a person I love, accept and appreciate. Accepting the past will allow you to focus on keeping your vibration high and making this world a better place.

Follow what lights you up

Your soul has a purpose. It has a mission to accomplish something in your lifetime through your physical being. It has a free will, and it's up to you and your soul how you choose to achieve its mission.

Your soul knows what it needs to do, and when you do something that excites you, you see this for yourself. When you feel happy, lit up by the work you do, the dreams you have or the people you surround yourself with, you feel your soul speaking through you. Your vibration moves to a higher frequency, and all of us on the earth benefit.

No doubt you've experienced days when you couldn't stop smiling, and moments when you've believed that anything is possible. When you feel like this, you walk along the street and people you meet pick up on your positive frequency and smile back. Even without you saying a word, people respond to you. In this state *anything* is possible. When you do what you love, when you follow your dreams, you send a powerful message to the world about yourself, and you give others permission to do the same. More than that, you inspire others, so they mirror your beautiful state.

Always follow what lights you up, and you will light up this world.

You are the citizen of the universe

You've reached the end of this book. I hope it has inspired you to begin your real adventure. The seed has been planted, and it's up to you to decide how to nurture it. I trust you'll do a wonderful job. I trust that we'll all see your true authenticity shining, and that we'll experience important shifts because of your work. We will all be proud and grateful. You can contribute to our awakening, help humanity and our entire existence. You are capable of creating incredible change. I have complete faith in you and don't doubt you, not for a second.

There's a reason why you found this book. By now, you'll know that it's time to get to work. Perhaps you've already started. There will be challenges, obstacles, distractions, doubts, fears, worries and conflicting voices. There will be people who try to lead you away from your path. Be aware of this, and don't let them do it. Acknowledge them and focus on what matters to you.

Remember that what you choose to focus on will expand. Work to handle every obstacle you encounter gracefully. Trust that you can create your own reality. You, and only you, are in charge. This is your truth. You choose what and who to believe, you choose what to discard. You have a vision and your vision is your mission. The universe gave you this mission because *only* you can fulfil it. Be brave, Mystic Butterfly. You're here to complete your mission and your soul will be here for eternity. There is nothing to fear, only things to experience.

Your life in its human form and your creations help to shape this world. Let your light be so bright that it will help others see the way to their truth too. You can do this, and I know you'll make the shift this earth and the whole unseen reality desires. I'm proud of you, and I send you off to your adventure.

This may seem like an impossible dream to you. But believe me, I really mean it. I'll continue doing my best to raise the consciousness of us all too. When you have good intentions, the support of others on the same frequency, and the higher wisdom which surrounds us, you will not fail. Your soul won't let you down. The truth of your soul is capable of dissolving the barriers which have been placed around the real cosmic oneness.

Shine your light upon them, so they become visible to us all. You are a child of the universe on a transformational journey on earth. You can learn to accept and love yourself, and in doing so, fly as high as you want. You can decide to do whatever you like with your life, using your free will and your infinite power. Beautiful Mystic Butterfly, spread your wings wide now and fly to the heights of the light where you meet your truth and make the world more beautiful and bright.

A thought to keep for eternity

'Let's make this experience on the earth a happy and fulfilling one, to help us reach a higher consciousness for ourselves, the planet and the entire universe.'

ACKNOWLEDGEMENTS

There are so many beautiful souls who have been supporting me on my journey. I want to thank you all. You know who you are and I am very honoured our paths have crossed in this time and space.

A special thank you goes to my mum and dad. Thank you for all your love, support and for always believing in me. I couldn't have asked for better parents. I love you so much.

I would also like to thank my sister, Maria. You are not only my sister in this physical reality, but a true soul sister I've known for lifetimes. You are so talented and inspiring in many ways. Thank you also for creating such beautiful artwork for this book's cover, which only your unique soul could channel. I love you.

A big thank you also goes to my brother-in-law, Dusan. I am so honored to call you my brother. Thank you for supporting me in every way and always recommending the best books to read.

Lots of love also goes to Sebastian, my nephew, and to Adele, my niece. You beautiful angels are my greatest teachers.

A huge thank you also goes to my best friend Anka. I am so proud to call you my friend. You constantly inspire me and I know I can rely on you one hundred percent.

A big thank you also goes to Paul. I am grateful for your friendship and our mysterious conversations no-one else understands. You're an amazing friend.

Another big thank you goes to my lovely friend Sam. You're my soul sister and I really appreciate all your support over the last few years. Thank you for being part of my life.

Thank you also to my dear friend Celine. You not only taught me to fly aeroplanes, you showed me how to embrace my fears and take responsibility for my life and my choices.

A massive thanks also goes to you, William. You are an amazing flying instructor. I learnt so much from you. You prepared me for all my navigation solo flights and my skills test beautifully. I'll always be grateful that you taught me how to become a safe and confident pilot. Thank you.

I am also deeply grateful to my dear friend and mentor Maxine. You taught me to find strength in my vulnerability. I learned so much from you on many levels. You are a true goddess and soul sister I will treasure for eternity.

Also thanks to my friend Martin for being there for me, especially when I reached the dark bottom of my life. Thank you for all your support and everything you've done over the years. I will always be thankful to you.

Thank you also to my friend Vladislav. You, my dear, have crossed over to the other side too early. I miss you every day and you will always stay in my heart. I want to thank you for believing in me. You were the biggest fan of *Mystic Butterfly*.

Thank you to my writing coach and editor Alice. Your literary skills, knowledge and your guidance has taught me so much.

Thank you also to Ellie, my amazing editor, for getting this book ready for publishing. You have done a wonderful job.

And to all my other lovely friends who had a huge impact on my life: Linda, Alex, Ginger, Roland, Pete, Richard, Boris and all of you I didn't mention. You are truly not forgotten.

A special thank you goes to you, my Soul. Thank you for choosing me to fulfill your mission here on earth.

Last, but not least, thank you too, dear reader for spending time with this book. I hope it gives you the guidance you're looking for and that it will continue to assist you on your journey of self-discovery and learning. I wish you great success on your journey. Do what brings the most joy to your soul and share your unique gifts with the world.

RECOMMENDED READING

There are many amazing teachers and authors whose work has influenced my personal journey and spiritual growth. I would like to thank them all from the bottom of my heart.

I'm listing some of their work in this recommended reading section. I believe they can inspire you too. Titles are in alphabetical order by author.

Bernstein, Gabrielle (2011). *Spirit Junkie*, Hay House UK.

Eadie, Betty J. (1995). *Embraced by the Light*. new edn. Element Books.

Ford, Debbie (2001). *The Dark Side of the Light Chasers*, Hodder & Stoughton.

Gawain, Shakti (2016). *Creative Visualization*. 40th edn. New World Library.

Hay, Louise (1984). *You Can Heal Your Life*. new edn. Hay House.

Jeffers, Susan (2007). *Feel the Fear and Do It Anyway*. 20th edn. Vermilion.

Jones, Anne (2002). *Heal Yourself*, Piatkus.

Peale, Norman Vincent (1990). *The Power of Positive Thinking*. new edn. Vermilion.

Simpson, Liz (2013). *The Book of Chakra Healing*. rev. edn. Sterling Publishing.

Tolle, Eckhart (2001). *The Power of Now*. 92nd edn. Yellow Kite.

ABOUT THE AUTHOR

Jana Prackova is a spiritual life coach and meditation teacher. Her mission in life is to assist others in finding their true potential, by living authentically and doing what they love.

Jana is also a private pilot and has been featured in the *LOOP* flying magazine and *The Flight School Times*, and has inspired many would-be pilots worldwide to follow their dreams.

In her spare time, she writes music and loves exploring the mysteries of the Universe.

Art By LAW Photography **www.mysticbutterfly.co.uk**

www.ingramcontent.com/pod-product-compliance
Lightning Source LLC
Chambersburg PA
CBHW070142080526
44586CB00015B/1811